STRONG SCHOOLS, STRONG LEADERS

WHAT MATTERS MOST IN TIMES OF CHANGE

Perry P. Wiseman

Rowman & Littlefield Education
Lanham • New York • Toronto • Plymouth, UK

Published in the United States of America
by Rowman & Littlefield Education
A Division of Rowman & Littlefield Publishers, Inc.
A wholly owned subsidiary of
The Rowman & Littlefield Publishing Group, Inc.
4501 Forbes Boulevard, Suite 200, Lanham, Maryland 20706
www.rowmaneducation.com

Estover Road
Plymouth PL6 7PY
United Kingdom

British Library Cataloguing in Publication Information Available

Library of Congress Cataloging-in-Publication Data

Wiseman, Perry P.
Strong schools, strong leaders : what matters most in times of change / Perry P. Wiseman.
p. cm.
Includes bibliographical references and index.
ISBN 978-1-60709-512-5 (cloth : alk. paper) – ISBN 978-1-60709-513-2 (pbk. : alk. paper) – ISBN 978-1-60709-514-9 (electronic)
1. Educational leadership. 2. School management and organization. 3. School improvement programs. I. Title.
LB2805.W545 2010
371.2–dc22 2009036460

∞™ The paper used in this publication meets the minimum requirements of American National Standard for Information Sciences–Permanence of Paper for Printed Library Materials, ANSI/NISO Z39.48-1992.
Manufactured in the United States of America.

This is for Samantha, Nick, Matthew,
and our newborn who will soon be arriving.
Samantha, you are the backbone of our family.
Kids, my purpose is to provide each of you
with a strong *foundation*
so you can have a prosperous life.

CONTENTS

FOREWORD

Strong Schools, Strong Leaders is an interesting book written by a school practitioner. Each chapter is filled with advice from a principal's perspective on how to successfully lead schools in the twenty-first century. Many of the ideas surround four essential "foundations" of leadership. They are: (1) listening to people and the environment, (2) building agreements, (3) co-creating purpose, and (4) fostering effective teams.

The most fascinating chapter is the first testimony of listening to people and the environment. This chapter adds to the theory base on leadership by emphasizing the importance of truly listening, not just data gathering. In a world filled with a lot of one-way communication, it is important to expand on the power of listening, both with our ears and our hearts. This book also contains a chapter containing specific strategies to aid listening, a meaningful addition to the theory.

The second foundation is that of building agreements. It merges Bruce Tuckman's theory of group development with the art of building productive norms by way of helping the practitioner to build agreements among various constituencies. Not only is this a valuable reminder that conflict is necessary in all organizations, but it is also a reminder that we must find ways to build agreements.

The third foundation is that of co-creating purpose. By now we should all surely know the importance of shared vision, mission, and purpose. But this book is unique in offering the reader a workshop to do just that. It poses a practical, hands-on approach to forming a shared vision by tapping into everyone's individual values and beliefs.

The fourth and last foundation is fostering effective teams. Building on the seventeen characteristics of effective teams that I developed with Bonita Drolet, this segment accurately depicts the characteristics and goes on to offer further strategies for building successful teams. This is a valuable addition to the teambuilding literature.

I recommend this book to you. Although many of the ideas are not unique to the literature on leadership, the intriguing use of "foundations" warrants a careful reading. It adds to our thought process on leadership.

Thomas R. Harvey
professor of organizational leadership,
doctorate program, University of La Verne, California
author/coauthor of *Checklist for Change*;
The Practical Decision Maker;
Building Teams, Building People;
The Politically Intelligent Leader

ACKNOWLEDGMENTS

First and foremost, I want to thank my mom, dad, and brother (Barbara, Bob, and Bobby). Each of you taught me the importance of values, family, and love. Without each of you, I would not be where I am today. I would also like to thank my mentor, Dr. Thomas Harvey, for taking me under his wing. You have always been there for me. I admire your honesty, leadership, and the ability to create a "healthy level of stress."

I want to give a special thanks to Dr. Larry Kemper for providing me some great feedback on my early drafts. You are always willing to lend a hand and I appreciate it. Finally, I want to thank the various school staffs that I have worked with over the years. You have made many of these ideas come to life. I look forward to the friendships that we will all continue to build.

1

STRONG SCHOOLS AND SOLID FOUNDATIONS

For a tree to become tall, it must grow tough roots among the rocks.

—Friedrich Nietzsche

These are tough times for schools. Everything is changing at a dizzying pace and the fact of the matter is many school leaders are finding it difficult to keep up. We have all seen better days. Yet, this is nothing new to us. Social, economic, and political change—or unsteadiness, depending on how one looks at it—has been with us for a long time. The pendulum will by no means stand still.

At this time, there are two glaring points about our current system no school leader can ignore. One, the United States government—presiding over the world's foremost economic engine—has accumulated a national debt of historic proportions, creating disarray in many of our schools. Two, the growing competition for resources and markets has become thoroughly interlocked, causing the world to become economically and socially integrated. Not only do our students now have to compete locally, but also with their peers from all over the world. The competition is far-reaching and global.

With each passing day, the unfolding dynamics place new demands, complications, and risks on school leadership. The challenge before school leaders today is not the unpredictability, which is recurrent and inevitable, but creating schools with the capacity to thrive no matter the state of affairs.

Schools with the aptitude to prosper during both the good and bad times are known as "strong schools." It does not matter whether unfolding political, economical, or social dynamics are in an upswing or not. The time to make a difference is now. The future rests on our ability to lead schools effectively.

Unfortunately, the easy solution in these trying times is for schools and leaders to cling to conventional approaches in the belief that they are "tried and true," or to take refuge in the latest school improvement fad. However, are these approaches sustainable? Some may be. Many will fail.

Quick-fix formulas are frequently unable to withstand many of the long-term challenges. Rather, they concentrate on cosmetic modifications to current and tired policy. This is not how schools should ride out the tough times, or *any* other type of circumstances. It's a sure-fire path to failure; successful school improvement is not, and has never been, simply about doing things the way they have always been done.

Employing a Christmas tree analogy, Michael Fullen (2001) explained that many schools "glitter from a distance—so many innovations, so little time—but they end up superficially adorned with so many decorations, lacking depth and coherence" (35–36). The new leader doesn't like to wander about, aimlessly searching for the latest fad. Leaders prefer to be alert and focused.

The focused transformation needed in our schools requires a type of leadership with the goal of not only growing successful, resilient schools, but also making them flourish in the face of distinctly new challenges. This need has created untold opportunities to develop a new model of dynamic leadership called the *foundational leader*. A foundational leader is precisely the type that can provide schools with the chance not merely to survive in unpredictable times, but also to thrive.

FOUNDATIONS IN EVERYDAY LIFE

One can consider education using an everyday example like planting a tree, which requires proper preparation of the soil, regular watering, mulching, and fertilizing to grow. Poor soil, no less than inclement weather, is likely to keep the seed from developing or the seedling from growing into a blossoming plant. When the soil is healthy, on the other hand, the roots grow strong enough to buckle sidewalks and the seedling should withstand natural adversity.

Here's another example. In order to lay the groundwork for a house, one has to grade a lot, assemble the pipes, configure the electrical wiring, and pour a cement slab, among other tasks. Done improperly, none of this work is likely to do much good. If the foundation is weak, the house becomes vulnerable to the elements.

How about raising children? Their basic values, beliefs, and worldviews take shape in the early years, influencing how they grow into adults. Yet, how many millions of children in the world live in unstable homes with poverty, abuse, violence, and family dysfunction? Their early experiences often sow the seed of suffering later in life—low self-esteem, substance abuse, and other problems. Short of a *foundational* upbringing, young adults are almost destined to stumble from one problem to another, to which too many already succumb.

Schools aren't much different in any of these respects.

FOUR KEY FOUNDATIONS FOR STRONG LEADERS

When one examines the continual "blossoming" of schools during demanding times, one finds that many schools have commonalities and share something. This "something" serves as the basis for keeping the schools sturdy. No matter how unstable the surroundings, there are still many schools that make significant increases in student achievement year after year. But how? What are the commonalities within and among these schools?

Four reasons are glaring. For one, their staff is more committed—as opposed to "compliant"—and their input is valued. Secondly, their staff behaves in a constructive manner and productive group norms emerge. Next, everyone's actions within the school community are aligned with a clear, compelling vision and values rooted in combined ideals and aspirations. Last, collaboration and teamwork bustle and it is clear that the staff has a detailed understanding of group dynamics.

These four characteristics serve as a starting point for constant school improvement, and without them, school leaders continue to wander without direction. They compose the *four key foundations*, and because the foundational leader's ambition is to create a successful, resilient school in the face of crises, he or she concentrates on these foundations, which can be summarized as:

- Foundation #1: Listening to People and the Environment
- Foundation #2: Building Agreements
- Foundation #3: Co-Creating Purpose
- Foundation #4: Fostering Effective Teams

The foundational leader is an agent of change who creates prosperous schools through explicit attention to each of the four key foundations. This new leader builds those foundations by facilitating a variety of processes that tap the collective wisdom of the entire school community.

The timing is perfect. Right now, our schools are in chaos. Intentions may be great, but have we really created school environments where the fundamental ingredients for authentic collaboration are in place?

HOW THIS BOOK IS ORGANIZED

Part I, "The Four Key Foundations for Strong Leaders," includes an in-depth discussion of each of the four fundamental foundations the foundational leader considers when making a school prosperous and collaboration-rich. Each foundational chapter in part I is followed by a chapter covering a selection of specific actions to make each foundation within reach for the practitioner. These foundations are the heart of building common ground within the school community.

Part II, "From Theory to Practice," articulates the foundational leader's vehicle for applying each of the four foundations. This consists of a school leadership approach revolving around *becoming a progressive practitioner.* This "progressive" approach will aid the initiation, implementation, and institutionalization of each of the four key foundations.

The final chapter, titled "Final Thoughts," serves as a call to action. Nowadays, few school leaders have the leisure to procrastinate. Time is of the essence. Building successful, resilient schools is a must–and now! Times are changing and so is school leadership. With each passing day, the knots of dysfunction are becoming more entangled.

WHAT THIS BOOK WILL DO FOR YOU

Many of the pieces discussed throughout this book are just common sense with which many school leaders may already be familiar. It's a bit like trying to get into shape or losing weight. There's no magic potion; it takes hard work and dedication, good diet and exercise. It takes both knowledge and discipline.

The same thing goes for building successful, resilient schools. It takes a laser-focused effort. The four key foundations must be the center of attention. If they are not, the traditional leader can grow tired, just spinning his or her wheels. Capacity must be built.

This book focuses not only on the theory behind each of the foundations, but also offers practical activities to help practitioners build on each of the foundations. Everyday examples are used throughout to explore ways in which educators can avail themselves of the foundational model.

It is important to note that many of these concepts parallel business leadership models because raising student achievement is not that far removed from improving profit margins; in both contexts, people have to work together to meet common goals. Leaders in the educational and business fields have no more and no less than the organized efforts of people with which to work, and the behavioral dynamics they face are remarkably similar.

I

THE FOUR KEY FOUNDATIONS FOR STRONG LEADERS

Do not worry if you have built your castles in the air. They are where they should be. Now put the foundations under them.

—Henry David Thoreau

INTRODUCTORY REMARKS

Part I centers on four all-so-critical foundations needed to build successful, resilient schools:

- Foundation #1: Listening to People and the Environment
- Foundation #2: Building Agreements
- Foundation #3: Co-Creating Purpose
- Foundation #4: Fostering Effective Teams

All four are essential to the school. Together, they determine if it, as a whole, has the capacity to reach new heights of achievement.

More specifically, they allow the foundational leader to build whole-school, not merely individual, capacity for change. Although these foundations–discussed separately in the chapters–are interconnected, they are also hierarchically structured.

Each chapter presents a conceptual model to assist in receiving, processing, and defining a particular foundation. These models illustrate the relationship among ideas, the school, and the real world. Together, they make up the basic conceptual framework within which the foundational leader functions.

2

FOUNDATION #1: LISTENING TO PEOPLE AND THE ENVIRONMENT

A wise owl sat on an oak; The more he saw the less he spoke; The less he spoke the more he heard; Why aren't we like that wise old bird?

—Unknown

The foundational leader listens to what the school has to say. The school is simply an abstraction, of course, so it can't speak of its own volition. However, it embodies a "collective intelligence," and mastering the art of listening to people and the environment helps the leader tap into the wealth of information and commitment of all the members of the school.

Listening is the bedrock foundation. In its absence, first, no school can hope either to survive or to develop; and second, none of the other three foundations can be laid. By listening, the foundational leader is open to information from every quarter and people from every station. An effective listener is also one who can communicate a readiness to hear both the members of the school and

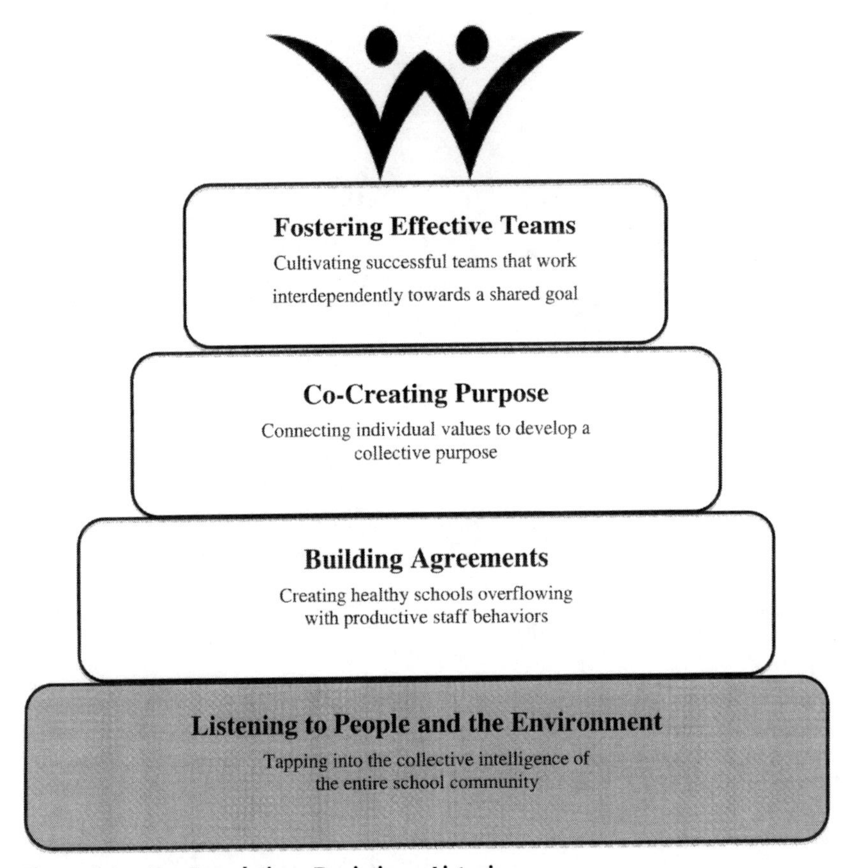

Figure 2.1. Key Foundations Depiction—Listening

the environment within which they work. Short of this communicative skill, any attempt to move the other foundations into place amounts to no more than cats chasing their tails.

TYPES OF LISTENING

Listening doesn't come easy; human nature leans more toward talking. The tendency is to speak and express ideas rather than to listen to others. Three leading influencers in the field of professional coaching, Laura Whitworth, Henry Kimsey-House, and Phil Sandahl

(1998) remarked, "To be listened to is a striking experience—partly because it is so rare. When another person is totally with you, leaning in, interested in every word, eager to empathize, you feel known and understood. People get bigger when they know they're being listened to; they have more presence. They feel safer and more secure, as well, and can begin to trust" (9). However, listening in social contexts cannot be overemphasized because building resilient schools actually starts when the leader listens to people and the environment rather than merely talking at them.

Hence, when listening, the foundational leader works diligently to pick up emotions, nonverbal cues, and the surrounding environment. This skill is necessary for building each of the remaining foundations that will be discussed in later chapters. Nonverbal cues give the foundational leader the intuition needed to facilitate change. As the foundational leader concentrates on building consensus, co-creating purpose, and fostering effective teams, he or she carefully listens to people and observes clues emerging from the environment.

LISTENING IN SCHOOLS

Listening in schools is essentially information gathering. For the foundational leader, two types of information gathering exist. The first deals with the information staff members engaged in large- or small-group processes routinely disclose to each other. At this level, the staff members desire to improve group norms, their sense of purpose, and the success of their respective teams. The foundational leader constantly refines this process by involving the members, especially the members of larger groups, in any change process.

People with the opportunity to offer input and lend a hand are more likely to support change. They are also more likely to be satisfied with decisions affecting their environment and more committed to the overall goals of their respective group.

The second type of information gathering pertains to what the foundational leader learns while taking time out to view activities "from the balcony," so to speak. This figure of speech stems from what Ronald Heifetz and Martin Linsky (2002) described as "getting off the dance floor and going to the balcony."

> Few practical ideas are more obvious or more critical than the need to get perspective in the midst of action. Any military officer, for example, knows the importance of maintaining the capacity for reflection, even in the "fog of war." Great athletes can at once play the game and observe it as a whole—as Walt Whitman described it, "being both in and out of the game." Jesuits call it, "contemplation in action." Buddhists call it "karma yoga," or mindfulness. We call this skill "getting off the dance floor and going to the balcony," an image that captures the mental activity of stepping back in the midst of action and asking, "What's really going on here?" (52)

All too often, traditional school leaders are caught up in the action, failing to see the dynamics unfolding right before their eyes.

For instance, at one school, one staff member was always devoted to the betterment of the school. More often than not, this particular individual would arrive early and leave late, running tirelessly to help fellow colleagues and students. Yet, as the year progressed, numerous complaints were launched about the staff member. This was far from typical.

After overhearing some complaints in the lunchroom, the staff member became enraged and wondered, "How could they betray me after everything I have done for this school?" Instead of addressing the concerns with colleagues, the individual disengaged from most school activities. Following that, rumors spread through the school like wildfire and the staff member's reputation quickly deteriorated.

"This is very unusual," the foundational leader might think when the root of the problem wasn't outright apparent. The complaints were widespread and bordering on nit picking.

What was the underlying behavior causing such a depressing situation? Was this particular staff member unable to build relationships with peers? Past actions painted a different picture, and when asked about relationships, the staff member replied, "I don't know why everyone is unhappy with me."

It was time for a foundational leader to look at the situation objectively without getting into a reactive mode, asking "What's really going on here?"

After some additional probing "from the balcony," something previously hidden became visible. In the months prior to the time complaints began rolling in, the individual made some poorly chosen comments to students about his relationship with a significant other. Though nothing graphic, the comments were not favorable for a classroom setting.

After hearing the remarks, each student shared them with other staff members throughout the school. The spreading of these remarks was comparable to bees traveling throughout a garden, cross-pollinating in the springtime.

The staff members who complained shared the same students with the individual. Everyone was upset and interpersonal relationships were spiraling downward. Even though the underlying cause wasn't noticeable at first, the environmental cues allowed the foundational leader to put two and two together.

Problem solved—well, not really. The foundational leader alerted the individual about being more cognizant of comments made in the classroom. Although the awareness could provide damage control for the future, the present situation was still difficult. Mending broken relationships among colleagues can be difficult; trust takes time to build but can be shattered in a heartbeat.

In schools, both disorderly and orderly times exist, but the foundational leader doesn't react in haste. Instead, he or she constantly moves to the balcony for a different angle on the situation. It's not impossible to change preconceptions if the foundations are sound with no hidden "agenda."

Listening to people and the environment is no mean task. Traditional school leaders operate autocratically in a command-and-control style, which tends to limit their view of the school. However, situations offer a time and a place for this style; for instance, when the safety of others is at risk. Should this be the case, the school leader must make decisions—and make them quickly, often without seeking staff input.

In everyday practice, the foundational leader operates by putting preconceptions aside and starting a learning curve anew by listening rather than talking down to staff members. Consideration must be given to the environment in which the opinions of the staff members are formed. The foundational leader knows implementing change requires participation by everyone, not just a select few.

The foundational leader knows change is facilitated through others and induced as an ongoing exchange between the leader and staff, which, in turn, motivates everyone to contribute successfully to the school or team. This foundation surrounds a model called "Listening to People and the Environment: A Balancing Process" (fig. 2.2). This listening model lends the foundational leader a hand in properly constructing the bedrock foundation.

LISTENING AS A PROCESS OF BALANCING

An integral caveat worth considering in the listening model is: Hearing too much of one thing can lead to misinterpretation and blurred judgment in problem-solving and decision-making. Such distortion is bound to create hurdles as the foundational leader moves to deal with the remaining three foundations. As the foundational leader listens to staff members and pays attention to the school environment from "the balcony," a sense of balance is created between two pulls.

In sum, a "balanced listening model" contains four critical components:

- Listening to people
- Paying attention to the environment
- Weighing urgency versus importance
- Asking the purpose

"Listening" within this framework determines the capability of the foundational leader to plan and make decisions. Collectively, the components are a bit like a thermostat, measuring the "tempera-

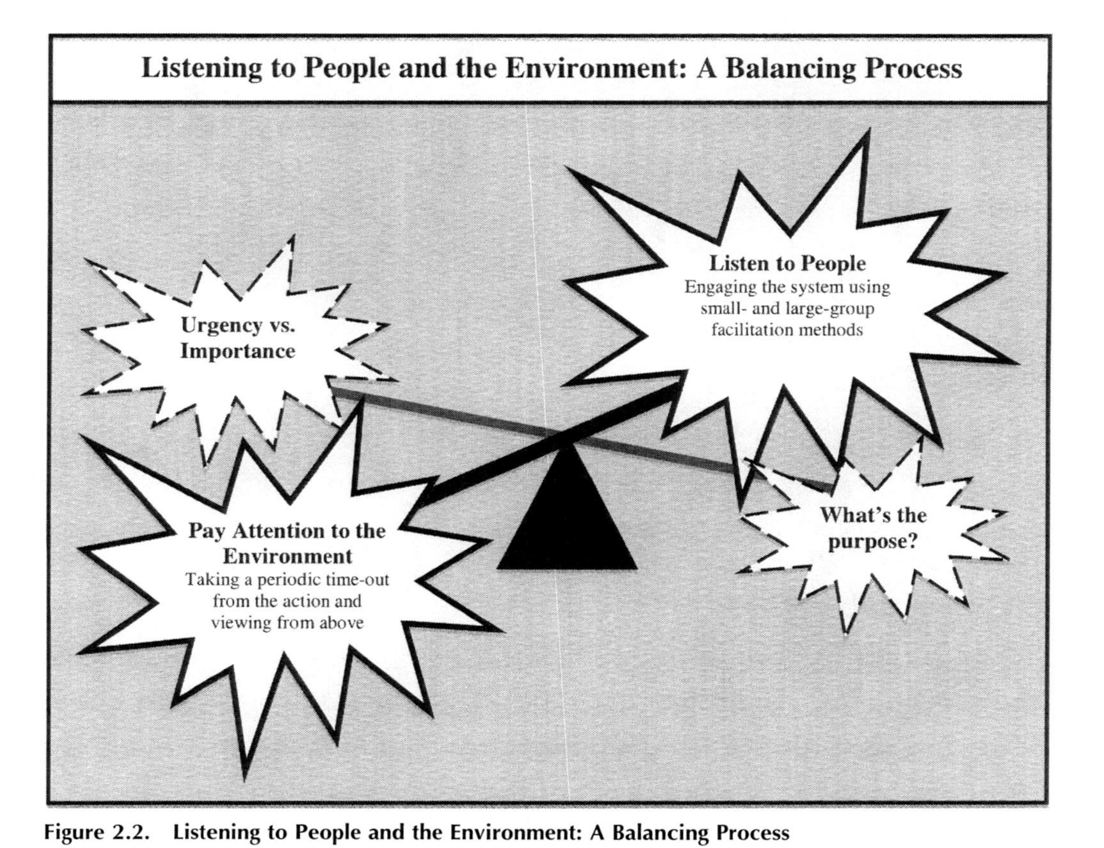

Figure 2.2. Listening to People and the Environment: A Balancing Process

ture" of the school. The question before the leader then becomes: Is it time to turn up the heat or cool it down?

Undue haste does not improve decisions. Taking time may. If the foundational leader reflects on the information coming from both people and the environment, it offers a surprisingly complete narrative for the school.

Decisions and change initiatives are weakened if information emanates solely from large- or small-group activities. Instead, information and themes must be also gathered from viewing the school through the "aerial lens" of the balcony. In addition, the aerial-view perspective has to be weighed against the input of each staff member. Both aspects are critical and must be given due consideration.

Listening to People

The primary goal of listening to people, the first component of this model, is to collect the perceptions of the school's members. This information is of incalculable importance. Too often, the traditional school leader makes major decisions without seeking the advice of those upon whom those decisions have the greatest impact. This is the mark of autocratic practice, a path so rife with roadblocks it can quickly defeat every change initiative in several ways.

First, listening, alone, conveys how the foundational leader intends to lead the staff members out of a dilemma. When members are invited to be a part of the solution and feel part of what they're helping to create, they tend to be much more motivated. Aside from the statistics supporting this view, it's just common sense. It's human nature to want to belong, and what better reason to belong than helping create. On the other hand, when significant decisions are imposed by the traditional leader, school members may find it easier to go through the motions than to carry them out properly.

Second, by involving others, the foundational leader applies a truth about the workplace we ignore at our peril: the greatest ideas often come, not from the loudest, but, sometimes, from those staff members who speak the least. Everyone counts. Who isn't familiar with meetings where those present fail to vocalize their ideas for a solution and, instead, vent a complaint or two? Instead of focusing on improvement, they want only to convey their views of what went wrong. The usefulness of this "complaint" exercise is limited. Sooner or later, it proves a waste of time.

Among those present are also staff members who, preferring to sit on the sidelines, listen patiently with little or no interest in offering anything new. They're all for change. Who's against change when things aren't right? And yet some of the most intelligent workers just sit on the fence waiting for the dust to settle.

Sterile meetings can be unnerving because the traditional leader may assume the few voices are truly representative. The foundational leader, on the other hand, finds a way to draw everyone into sharing and contributing their ideas. A norm is established—accompanied by inclusive processes—whereby everyone should expect an opportunity to express ideas. Staff members feel free to offer insight and even a global view of the situation. In return, gratitude is expressed to everyone.

The foundational leader not only thrives on differences, he or she translates diversity into a collective intelligence surpassing the wisdom of any given individual.

Staff members have ideas to offer. One of the main reasons they don't is often fear. Some are concerned about a dominant member, while others fear a rival may shoot down their ideas. Whatever the obstacles, no leader can afford to neglect this important source of information and it should never be assumed the tight-lipped lack ideas.

The foundational leader confronts feelings of helplessness head-on, perhaps by crafting future meeting designs to invite, not discourage, participation.

An example can be a straightforward meeting where pertinent information about a particular system for monitoring student behavior needs to be disseminated. To date, few members of the school have had an opportunity to share their perceptions of ways in which to improve the system. However, everyone sitting in the room has a responsibility for implementation.

Two options are available. The first is to argue the need for a new system, present it, answer questions, and expect magic to happen.

Unfortunately, frequently using this method could result in the magical appearance of a tomato—flying right toward someone's head.

The second approach is to present the monitoring system and give the members of the school an opportunity to generate ideas to enhance its effectiveness. This can be as easy as offering everyone a few minutes following the presentation to write ideas anonymously on an index card, sharing concerns and possible solutions. Or the participants can be broken into smaller groups to discuss improving the upcoming system, followed by sharing with the whole group.

Of course, the foundational leader chooses the latter approach whenever possible because of a relentless attitude that *we are smarter than me*. Some of the ideas can be used and others discarded. Either way, at least the members' ideas were solicited.

Yet, listening to people is not a one-way street. It takes forethought and work on the part of both the leader and the members of the school. The foundational leader is in command of a process maximizing the contribution to ideas. And it is made known those ideas have to be narrowed down to a handful of options.

Paying Attention to the Environment

The dynamics unfolding within schools speak loudly. It is important for the foundational leader not only to focus on group processes in listening to people, but also to everything else emerging. The environment has something to say and it is not always common knowledge.

An example can be a team struggling with interpersonal relationships. From the leader's seat, it might look like this team is working cohesively—like a "well-oiled machine." Yet, the reality is one of the members is having difficulty listening to others because he talks too much. Each team meeting is filled with one-way conversation, taking up everyone's precious time. No one else has the opportunity to express his or her viewpoints and opinions.

Although his behavior is having a negative effect on team morale, the rest of the team is reluctant to confront his passive-aggressive behavior openly. Whenever the leader asks, "How's the team doing?" the usual response is, "Things are going great." No one is willing to disclose the faults of the team member in question, fearing both possible personal repercussions and an unsympathetic reaction by the leader.

In time, the flow of fresh ideas slows down considerably. Although the members comply with "team" decisions, they are not loyal to those decisions. By then, the foundational leader is beginning to see the quality of the team's tasks and commitment deteriorating. Although the information coming from the people is saying one thing, the environment is saying another. This calls for an intervention.

No one is better placed than the foundational leader to detect the collectively unseen—and perhaps unconscious—motivations driving a school's members. There has to be a root cause why this or that staff member is failing to meet the supervisor's expectations.

It may not be easy initially to distinguish questions of motivation from those of ability; however, as soon as an individual or team shows signs of dysfunction, the foundational leader must explore the unit's environment and check for the hidden causes of the dysfunction. A foundational leader attaches a strong sense of personal responsibility to internal challenges, whatever they may be. An instinct for sound solutions is developed. The slightest dysfunction in the school calls for a response, which empowers the afflicted staff members to resume their path toward realizing their full potential by using their own strengths.

Paying attention is about digging deeper and asking: "What is really going on here?" Posing this question in order to investigate—in effect, listening even more intently—brings the foundational leader closer to what the school as a whole is saying in both words and deeds.

As the old adage goes, a picture is worth a thousand words. When thought alone hasn't brought the foundational leader to a realization, it is time to put a pen to paper, sketching the unfolding dynamics of the school. What do these dynamics look like? Where are they coming from? Doodling on a piece of paper may seem rudimentary; nonetheless, it gives a chance for quiet reflection.

Michael Michalko's (2006) *Thinkertoys: A handbook of creative-thinking techniques* can get the inventive juices flowing again and aid understanding of complex dynamics. It's an ingenious guide suggesting some unconventional approaches to helping the foundational leader make the invisible visible.

For example, Michalko offers a technique described as "Think Bubbles." This procedure can be used for dynamics that defy understanding. The impressions and thoughts about the dynamic are mapped out in a particular fashion and studied intently. Once no further ideas emerge, the "map" is put away for a few days. Upon returning to it, a moment of insight usually occurs, followed by an interval of focused thought. This is just one of the ways the foundational leader "goes to the balcony," leading to those *ah-ha!* moments and a better understanding of the hidden connections.

Weighing the Important versus the Urgent

As the foundational leader considers the information obtained by listening to both the members of the school and environment, the information is digested and it is determined whether it pertains to an important or an urgent matter.

Depending on the time scale, both important and urgent matters require a different type of listening, followed by the appropriate response. If it is "important" but not urgent, a method and ample opportunity should be provided for people to be part of the change. The "Important versus Urgent Matrix" (fig. 2.3) displays a matrix the foundational leader uses when determining when and whom to involve in the decision-making process.

What about a memo delivered to all leaders in the school requesting a report due first thing the next morning? Is this matter important or just urgent?

The deadline alone makes it urgent. Time takes precedence. Is it also important? Perhaps not. It's likely the report will not make or break the school. Is there a need to call an emergency meeting to get the input of each and every staff member? Maybe, maybe not. The close deadline shows the report assumes the information for the leader is easily accessible. If the report suggests a possible impact on the future of the school, the foundational leader is well advised to

	Important	Not Important
Urgent	**Urgent and Important** Seek input from key stakeholders	**Urgent and Not Important** Seek input from those that possess information necessary to complete the task
Not Urgent	**Not Urgent and Important** Seek input from everyone	**Not Urgent and Not Important** Seek input from those that possess information necessary to complete the task

Figure 2.3. Important versus Urgent Matrix

obtain input from all staff members. The foundational leader might develop a quick, ten-minute, online survey of all the staff members who may be affected by the report. This is a seamless way to get all the relevant facts for an informed decision.

Another example could be a proposal for a new schoolwide math program for the subsequent school year. In this case, the approach involves much more than a quick report due the following day. The foundational leader recognizes an opportunity to listen to people because the flow of information compels a suitability judgment of the program, not to mention the specific steps for its implementation.

A whole-scale program imposed on the members of the school without proper hearing leads to trouble down the road. Thus, the decision is vital, not urgent, and the foundational leader has time to bring everyone together behind a plan. This done, a systematic approach to gathering and prioritizing thoughts along the way can develop.

Finally, the foundational leader gleans information by viewing the school "from the balcony." It may point to a problem, like a staff member who has trouble meeting deadlines. It's possible this individual's team has imposed too many tasks on him or her, and the team's responsibilities have not been equitably distributed. This can be detrimental to the team's overall performance. The leader has to intervene. Only, an adverse effect on results and relationships has made the problem both urgent and important. The foundational leader has to bring together key stakeholders and facilitate processes to produce a more equitable distribution of the work.

What's the Purpose?

So far, the discussion of the balancing model has surrounded two processes: balancing the information obtained from the school members and the environment in which they operate and weighing what is urgent and what is important. What hasn't been mentioned is the purpose guiding all this.

The foundational leader doesn't collect information for its own sake; there is a purpose:

1. Is the purpose of gathering information to widen an existing knowledge base?
2. Is the purpose to solve complicated problems?

The answers to these questions guide activities and all subsequent actions taken by the foundational leader.

For example, if, in a particular school, the information gathered through formal and informal observations (paying attention to the environment) speaks to a need for more focused strategies in the classrooms, then the foundational leader's purpose is to gather information to add to the existing knowledge base on best practices for these specific strategies.

This can be handled in a couple of ways. A traditional leader can employ the stand-and-deliver approach to present distinct strategies and expect them to emerge in each classroom, but it might not be the best method to gather information. The information gathered in that manner is the grumblings of staff members in response to imposed strategies.

The second method (the foundational leader's approach) could be to provide time for groups of individuals to work in concert and create their own strategies and best practices. Again, the *we are smarter than me* attitude kicks in. Next, each group shares its one most promising strategy with the rest of the staff. Perhaps, the foundational leader suggests each staff member vote on two or three presentation strategies most beneficial to the school. The leader listened to the people and they were consequently more likely to make the most of the strategies.

Another example includes the gathering of information to make key decisions or solve complex problems. The purpose is to gather and winnow an assortment of new and old ideas—nurturing everyone's mixture of experiences and expertise—to enhance some system or program. In this case, the foundational leader is meticulous in designing in-depth meetings where everyone can brainstorm, engage in deep dialogue, and share.

HEARING AND BALANCING THE VOICES

Imagine a professional boxing match going into the twelfth round. Both athletes sit exhausted in their respective corners, while the sold-out crowd is clamoring for a decisive finish. The bell rings, the boxers quickly touch gloves, and one boxer's corner man yells, "Get to the inside and jab. Stay away from the ropes." However, the arena is filled with so much noise, his voice barely registers.

Is the corner man wasting his time? Not if the athlete can hear him, and he does. He has spent countless hours of training doing just that. His coach shouts and screams, day in, day out; thus, when the time comes, the boxer is able to tune out the din around him and listen to one voice only. The same happens in almost every other spectator sport. Athletes have an amazing ability to focus on the single, guiding voice of their coach.

Unlike the athlete, the foundational leader listens to as many voices as possible. This special talent rests on how well the leader maintains a sense of balance amid the information and ideas flowing from disparate sources, including many kinds of facts and perhaps several, even contradictory, versions of the same facts. If the foundational leader listens to only one, the message may be distorted. The foundational leader dispassionately views all the relevant facts and asks, "What's really going on here?"

Whenever information is received—either by processes intended to generate ideas from others (listening to people) or by observation of the "unfolding dynamics" (paying attention to the environment)—the foundational leader determines which interventions need to be put into place and how quickly. As the information flowing in from people and the environment is balanced, the foundational leader understands the importance of having to *go slowly in order to go fast.* Time is a perennial concern, and too many leaders resort to the traditional style in their decision-making because of it. Unfortunately, this style causes them to spend even more time on the back end, cleaning up the incorrectly implemented pieces.

Spending the necessary time upfront during the planning stages and giving others the opportunity to share their knowledge, ideas, and strengths leads to more efficient decisions and change efforts. It's paradoxical, to be sure, but the foundational leader knows how to avoid being entangled in time-consuming command-and-control relationships. The foundational leader thrives on a participative style from the outset, generating more and more ideas, because he or she wants to do it right the first time.

3

METHODS FOR "LISTENING": CREATING COMBINED WISDOM IN SCHOOLS

Effective questioning brings insight, which fuels curiosity, which cultivates wisdom.

—Chip Bell

In a nutshell, foundational leaders listen to their school in order to make better-informed decisions. Listening also empowers the school members to take ownership in the midst of change initiatives. Relying on the group, whose collective intelligence surpasses the brainpower of any single individual, creates wisdom. The foundational leader makes every effort to involve others.

This chapter introduces five methods leaders can use when listening to the people through group processes in a climate of change. In addition, specific resources are provided to help school leaders invoke participation.

CHAPTER 3

A DIVERSITY OF MEETING DESIGNS TO INVOKE PARTICIPATION

Meeting designs can take a variety of shapes and forms. The goal of the foundational leader is to expand these designs so they stray from the traditional stand-and-deliver approaches. This method isn't exciting for participants and it contradicts the foundational leader's charge of listening to the people.

Structured meeting formats using effective techniques allow the leader to successfully obtain information on complex problems from several people. And foundational leaders have a pocketful of these approaches. This new leader is skilled in the practice of facilitation, inducing rich dialogue and creative ideas.

The foundational leader must have the ability to bring the group's wealth of knowledge to the surface. The task in developing efficient meeting design is to help the group increase effectiveness by improving how they work together, leading to ideas that are more inventive.

In his extensive book titled *The Ultimate Training Workshop Handbook*, Bruce Klatt (1999) spoke of the weight of listening to others and involving them in the process through meeting formats. He claimed this collective experience was at the heart of leadership: *Democratic Process + Results = Leadership.*

In due course, results achieved without involvement can lead to bitterness and a lack of buy-in. Once employees disengage, it is difficult to sustain results. With that in mind, school leaders aiming for sustainability ought to seek techniques to help facilitate participation.

Following are five easy techniques to assist in meeting design and induce participation:

Technique #1: Nominal Group Technique

Nominal Group Technique is a simple method to generate ideas with everyone having an equal voice. Each of the steps is represented below:

1. The facilitator presents the problem or decision.
2. The facilitator tells the group they have a few minutes to think about the problem or decision.
3. The facilitator has the individuals silently generate and write their ideas on 3x5 cards.
4. The facilitator gathers the ideas from each individual in a round-robin style and records them on a chart. When working with a large number of individuals, various groupings can be assigned.
5. When all ideas have been recorded, the group discusses each idea in order until everyone has a common understanding. If the group is large, the members can divide into smaller groups to collaborate and collectively share information on and merits and demerits of each idea.
6. With group agreement, the facilitator eliminates duplicate ideas and combines similar ones. (Harvey, Bearley, and Corkrum, 2001)

Technique #2: Mind Mapping

Mind mapping offers time for groups to analyze complex problems by organizing their thoughts.

1. Participants examine a problem following a brainstorming session. Starting at the center of a flipchart page, they write a word or phrase that accurately frames the topic or focal point of the mind map.
2. Without worrying about logical levels, order, or relationships, and using only single words or brief phrases, participants add all related information to the page.
3. Participants draw connections among ideas as they are listed.
4. Participants work until all possible elements or issues have been exhausted.
5. In the next step, categories are color-coded to show additional relationships.

6. Participants may need to redraw the mind map to reorganize the categories and to improve the visual of relationships and connections among elements. (Harvey, Bearley, and Corkrum, 2001)

Technique #3: Storyboarding

This method allows groups to visualize, prioritize, and capture ideas.

1. Write the group problem in large letters on an oversized piece of paper. Post the paper in the upper left-hand corner of the workspace. In the upper right-hand corner, post another paper containing the group's desired outcome.
2. The group should brainstorm topic headings, placing them on the header cards between the problem and outcome cards.
3. As the group continues brainstorming and posting ideas and tasks under each header, have them sequence the tasks under each heading.
4. The facilitator aids the group in reviewing the posted work and checking for missing major steps or tasks.
5. Using additional sticky notes or writing on the task cards, specific duties are assigned to individuals within the group.
6. Ask a volunteer to record the completed storyboard.

Technique #4: Spend a Dot

This method narrows or prioritizes a number of items on a list.

1. Record the possible solutions or ideas on a chart or series of charts and post the chart(s) on a wall.
2. Give each participant a set number of colored dots. The number of dots should be approximately 20 or 30 percent of the total number of ideas posted, and should not exceed ten dots.
3. Advise each participant to place one or all of the dots next to an item or items he or she considers important.
4. Count the number of dots for each item.

5. Discuss the implications of each item with the group. (Harvey, Bearley, and Corkrum, 2001)

Technique #5: Strengths, Weaknesses, Opportunities, and Threats (S.W.O.T.)

This method identifies and organizes information about the strengths, weaknesses, opportunities, and threats a group or idea may be facing.

1. Split the participants into two groups. One group discusses internal strengths and weaknesses, while the other group discusses external opportunities and threats.
2. Draw four columns on the workspace, labeling them: *Strengths*, *Weaknesses*, *Opportunities*, and *Threats*.
3. Bring the groups together to report their discussions.
4. Record each group's ideas under the corresponding headings on the chart.
5. Close by asking three questions to help the group process the information.
   a. What stands out?
   b. What surprises you?
   c. What can the group do with this information?

OPEN-SPACE TECHNOLOGY

Any leader wishing to bring groups of employees together (no matter the size) to address complex issues has to, at some time, draw on a process called "open space technology" (OST). This is a remarkable way to listen to people and the environment.

This innovative process does not require extensive planning on the part of the leader. OST is a self-organizing process wherein the participants actually construct the agenda, meeting times, and places.

"Hold on a minute," states the traditional leader. "How can we expect to tackle complex issues during a meeting when there is no set agenda?"

Every leader has the same uneasy feeling the first time he or she practices OST. However, the hundreds of thousands of individuals who have been through this inventive process would offer the leader three words of advice: Trust the process.

Harrison Owen (1997a and 1997b), the originator of the meeting structure OST, worked on the topic for a twelve-year period with thousands of people from four continents. The conception of OST developed from Owen's observations of the indescribable energy during coffee breaks at an international conference in 1983. He posed the following question: "Was it possible to combine the level of synergy and excitement present in a good coffee break with the substantive activity and results characteristics of a good meeting?" (1997a, 3). Through his efforts, a simple, fun, and productive process was born—OST. Although uncomplicated, the method is designed to tackle major issues, which increase in complexity. It is also appropriate for urgent and important issues.

The initial meeting space for OST consists of all participants sitting in circles or in concentric circles for larger groups. According to Owen (1997a), the application of circles equaled the fundamental geometry of open communication. Following a brief opening, the leader introduces the Situation that Needs Attention (SITNA) or theme of the event. This sets the stage for the next step when employees are given the opportunity to take ownership in bettering the situation. Following an overview of the task-at-hand, the leader invites anyone to identify an issue surrounding the SITNA and to take personal responsibility for convening a brainstorming workshop on the issue to generate ideas and possible solutions.

It is truly surprising to see how many participants step up to the plate when they are given the opportunity to make a difference. Each person offering to convene a brainstorming workshop is asked to come to the center of the circle, write the issue on a large piece of paper, announce the issue, meeting time, and meeting place to the group, and post it on the wall.

Once each convener has identified and posted all issues, the leader provides direction or *ground rules* for the remainder of the process. Particularly, the leader talks about the "Principles of Open

Space Technology" and the "Law of Two Feet." Owen (1997a, 95–99) describes each principle and the law as follows:

Principle #1: Whoever comes are the right people.

What counts is not how many people come, or even who comes (in the sense of status or position), rather the quality of the interaction and conversation make the difference. For good conversation, the convener and others only need one other person who shares their passion.

Principle #2: Whatever happens is the only thing that could have.

Real learning and real progress take place only when one moves beyond his or her original agendas and convention-bound expectations. If things turned out just the way everyone expected, life would be exceedingly dull, and learning, in any useful sense, simply would not occur. Growth occurs precisely in moments of surprise, large and small. It is important to cherish such moments and realize whatever happens is the only thing that could have.

Principle #3: Whenever it starts is the right time.

This principle serves as an important notice about the nature of creativity and spirit. Both are essential and neither pay much attention to the clock. They appear (or not) in their own time, which, by definition, means it is the right time. Thus, all parties need to be advised that just because a meeting is scheduled for 3:00 p.m., there is absolutely no guarantee anything useful will take place at the exact moment. Whenever it starts is the right time.

Principle #4: When it's over, it's over.

This principle offers a marvelous way to save time and aggravation. If a group gets together and it takes ten minutes to do what they wanted, congratulations. Move on and do something else. If on the other hand, they find themselves deeply engaged in what they are doing, they keep doing it until it is completed.

The Law of Two Feet

The only law states that if, during the course of the gathering, people find themselves in a situation in which they neither learn nor contribute, they must engage their two feet and go to a more productive place.

The next to last step—following the announcement of the principles and law—is for each participant to walk up to the wall and sign up for the issues they find of interest. From this point forward, the event is self-managing.

At the conclusion of the event, each convener shares the ideas and findings with the entire group. This is often in the form of handouts outlining ideas generated in the workshops. If time permits, these issues can be prioritized, possible "next steps" can be established, and perhaps can be presented to higher ups for more informed decision-making. Either way, an OST event brings about a slew of new perspectives and ideas to benefit the school.

At one particular school, the principal sought contributions from her employees on improving their tiered intervention system to meet the needs of at-risk students. Of course, she exercised the traditional method of creating a leadership team (e.g., department chairs, team leaders, and others) to discuss the topic; however, the issue was becoming a priority that required the attention of the entire staff. Everyone needed to be involved because a major overhaul of the school's instructional programs had the potential to affect all stakeholders.

After hearing of OST, the principal decided to try the method. Although hesitant at first because of the lack of control, she made the decision to move forward. Little did she know, the OST event would be the makings of a complex tiered intervention system that did not allow any student to fall through the cracks. The new program was formed by input from everyone in the school.

Before moving to the next method, it is noteworthy to share the significance of the input generated during an OST process. The foundational leader understands that if the school members participate in this idea-generating process, the ideas have to be applied in some way. If they participate and the leader rejects their ideas, trust is broken and commitment is lost. A lack of follow through ensures they feel as if their ideas were not heard. Following OST, participants are re-energized. It is something powerful and different.

Anyone interested in open space technology should consider Owen's works titled *Open Space Technology: A User's Guide* (1997a) and *Expanding Our Now: The Story of Open Space Technology* (1997b).

SEARCHING ADDITIONAL SOURCES ON LARGE-GROUP PROCESSES

A wealth of information is available on the methods of engaging school members in large- and small-group meetings. If the foundational leader is to master the art of facilitating change, it is important he or she become familiar with this information through various sources. Here are some good references:

- *The Change Handbook* by Peggy Holman, Tom Devane, and Steven Cady (2007). Sixty-one different change methods are offered by the originators and leading practitioners in the field.
- *The Practical Decision Maker* by Thomas Harvey, William Bearley, and Sharon Corkrum (2001). This resource includes fifty-four different structuring devices for problem solving.
- *Large Group Interventions* by Barbara Bunker and Billie Alban (1997). This book demonstrates a variety of interventions to create commitment from everyone.
- *The Handbook of Large Group Methods* by Barbara Bunker and Billie Alban (2006). Similar to their earlier work in *Large Group Interventions*, Bunker and Alban provide a comprehensive overview of newer methods to apply.

Through persistent study, practice, and reflection the foundational leader can be better prepared for the ongoing pursuit of building successful, resilient schools. This feat cannot be accomplished with old tricks. A new, extensive toolbox of processes to engage the entire system must be established.

ONLINE SURVEY TOOLS

Online survey tools are great for gathering information quickly from people throughout the school. Many low-cost websites allow users to create professional survey formats to be turned into customized surveys with multiple choices, drop-down menus, and comment boxes. These surveys can be sent out to the members of the school.

Some widely used online resources automatically offer reports summarizing the gathered data, including SurveyMonkey.com, Zoomerang.com, and Checkbox.com. In one school, the principal regularly facilitated an inclusive series of meetings where staff could share input about successful change. However, the principal also designed an online survey to gather input because contractual issues did not allot enough time for face-to-face meetings. As a foundational leader, the principal combined sporadic e-mails with the online survey. Everyone was positive about the process because it related to a number of important decisions.

Online surveys are simple and effective. On urgent or important issues, the foundational leader needs the insight of staff before committing to a decision. Bringing everyone together takes time and effort, and does not always allow for face-to-face meetings. Taking a couple of minutes to complete an online survey is far less disruptive.

SURROUNDING ONESELF WITH INFORMAL LEADERS

Vital Smarts is a consulting firm offering a variety of seminars on themes like Crucial Conversations, Crucial Confrontations, and the Influencer. At a seminar on the Influencer, the presenters spoke about informal opinion leaders. Because they are well respected by their peers, informal leaders exert influence, allowing them to sway the opinions of others. The foundational leader has to discover the informal leaders in the school and keep them close to any change initiative.

This can be accomplished by sending an anonymous questionnaire asking the following: "Of all the staff members in the school, whose opinion do you most respect?" This questionnaire can be distributed either at the next staff meeting or online. Tallying and scoring the names of individuals should reveal the three to five most influential opinion leaders. Once established, the foundational leader can make a habit of calling them informally to talk about the change process or other ideas about how to improve the school. Because they are kept close for advice, they are enlisted as the most effective agents of change in the school. The informal leaders are the pulse of the school and the foundational leader should listen intently to the opinions of these leaders.

4

FOUNDATION #2: BUILDING AGREEMENTS

People's behavior makes sense if you think about it in terms of their goals, needs, and motives.

—Thomas Mann

Transformation in schools has the potential to produce unwanted conflict, often leading to ineffective processes, reduced communication, and poor working relationships. It is a fact of life. Change brings about tension and without managing the behaviors of individuals and the school as a whole, leaders see their school's ability to succeed plummet.

The impact is exponential. While each staff member's actions, inactions, and interactions shape the environment of the school, their cumulative effect can have much more dramatic results.

When it comes to inherent tensions hindering progress of the school, the leader can take two approaches. For one, the leader can aim a BB gun line of attack by relentlessly documenting persons demonstrating patterns of sub-par behavior, ultimately leading to

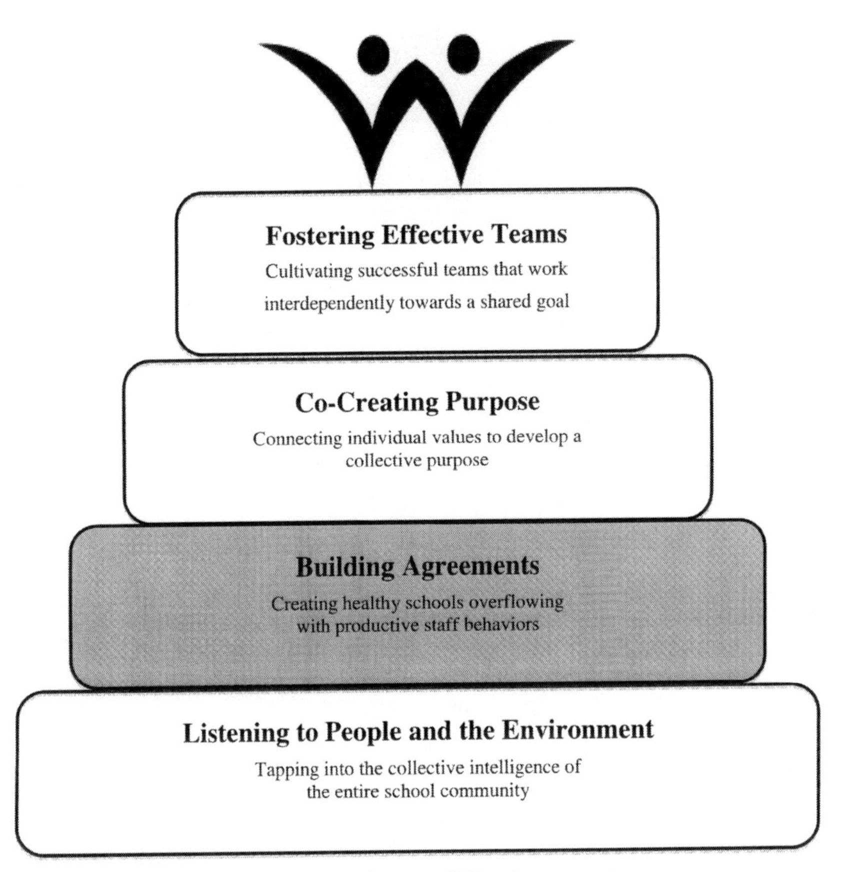

Figure 4.1. Key Foundations Depiction—Building Agreements

disciplinary action. Word will get around that certain behavior is not tolerated, and most members of the school will get the hint. Yet, without a well-known set of "rules," this approach creates more stress within the school. It may even push many staff members to stray away from working with others for fear of disciplinary action if things go badly in their own day-to-day dealings.

The second option, building agreements, can be linked to a shotgun approach. In effect, it is far-reaching and effective, yet it doesn't dismiss those who are already doing things right. Building agreements is about the leader making a deliberate effort to engage the entire staff in the creation of shared and accepted expectations for staff behavior. In other words, the members of the school proactively develop and agree upon productive norms. These norms serve as the staff's commitments to act or behave in certain ways. Once these agreements are in place, a whole-school reward exists and everyone is able to turn conflict and tension into progress.

Building agreements is the second of the four key foundations. It creates a whole-school capacity to prevail over the natural conflict accompanying change. This foundation is interrelated with the first foundation, listening to people and the environment. First, the foundational leader has to pay close attention to the environment and try to untangle the precise tensions stirring throughout the school. When the tensions are viewed "from the balcony," the leader is better able to find the root cause of the conflict. Perhaps, the tensions are rooted in disjointed lines of communication between individuals. These tensions could even stem from the way various staff members speak to one another. Whatever the tensions may be, they have to be undraped, made public, and addressed openly.

The second connection is the leader's ability to constantly listen to the people and give them leeway to create their own set of shared expectations for behaviors bound by productive norms. Once ideals and principles come to life, members of the school begin to hold one another accountable for the fulfillment of expected behaviors. Shared accountability is the fundamental goal of building agreements because peer pressure is much more powerful than the leader twisting arms.

Spending the necessary time to eliminate any ambiguity in expected behaviors is far from wasteful when the aim is to provide a concise guide for individual and collective behavior. A systematic approach guarantees, above all, that everyone recognizes the values they share as a group. Explicitly developed productive norms have the advantage of helping the members of the school deal consciously and conscientiously with any situation before it begins to impede progress.

The best way is to be proactive and lay a solid foundation to help manage negative behavior. The foundational leader creates an environment in which productive behaviors thrive because the environment determines how the school members behave. For this, the foundational leader establishes the structures and processes leading to productive behaviors—building agreements.

EVERYDAY EXAMPLES OF TENSION IN SCHOOLS

Consider three different examples of conflict in schools and how they determine *the way things are done around here.* While reading each example, think about the following question: Could any specific action, inaction, or interaction have prevented each of these circumstances?

Example #1: "I Quit!"

This first example is about two staff members working on a special project past normal school hours. Both are passionate about the project, and the extra money is also appreciated with the holidays nearing. They have separate responsibilities requiring few face-to-face contacts, allowing them instead to communicate with each other by telephone or e-mail.

The relationship begins to sour one day when an e-mail message is misconstrued. They mention their current difficulty to other staff members, who subsequently become involved and take sides. As time goes on, the relationship deteriorates to a point where one of the two employees informs the leader (who still isn't aware of the conflict) that interest in the project has come to a halt and the leader needs to find someone else to take over the responsibilities.

These staff members allowed their conflict to fester until one of them gave up. Their failure to repair the trust adversely affected the project and the school.

Example #2: "A Late Start"

The next story is familiar to all. A particular school has staff meetings every Monday at 2:30 p.m. One rainy Monday afternoon, people trickled into the meeting room—late. It was already 2:34 p.m., but the school's leader ignored everyone's tardiness and continued to converse privately with one or two people. By the time everyone was ready to begin, it was already 2:36 p.m.

This conveys a two-fold message to the group. First, "Around here, we don't start meetings on time"; and second, "To all who are seated and ready on time, your time is not valuable." After a few more months of tardiness, some in the latter group felt so underappreciated that other problems erupted, ultimately leading one key staff member to walk out.

Example #3: "Rumors"

The last example has endless boundaries because sometimes personal and professional lives do blend. One school had an exceptionally difficult week due to school wide testing, four student assemblies, and a fire drill. The winds blowing all week did not help. This host of atypical activities, accompanied by gusts, produced hyperactivity in the students. By Friday afternoon, everyone was exhausted.

To unwind from the week, eight staff members went to a local bar and grill for food and drinks. After appetizers and a few cocktails, the group was having a grand old time. As the night evolved so did the conversation. It started with harmless venting and unfortunately progressed to mockery of fellow school members who were not present.

By the next week, the banter from the evening began to whisper its way through the school. Opinions and perceptions were being formed. Loose lips sink ships.

What Could Have Prevented These Circumstances?

These three examples are commonplace in schools. They particularly illustrate how lack of awareness can allow seemingly trivial events (actions, inactions, and interactions) to create tensions that pose a serious barrier to school progress.

Was it possible for the leaders of these schools to discern what was going on sooner? How would they go about trying to find out?

After all, the leader cannot be everywhere and know everything all the time, and many pitfalls lie hidden from view.

From the perspective of the foundational leader, one specific "inaction" led to adversity in each of the examples: the failure to bring all members of the school together to proactively create and agree upon norms. Without these agreements, each of the staff members in the examples was seafaring without a compass. They did not have a common set of principles to which to cling when confronting the issues.

Why People Do What They Do

Human behavior is multifaceted and complex. Some behaviors are acceptable; others are not. Bad behavior in schools takes a variety of forms: unprofessional e-mails, team members not conscientious enough to complete their tasks, verbal altercations, uncommunicativeness, nonverbal cues, denial of support, rumor mongering–the list is endless.

Why, then, do school members sometimes exhibit behaviors that compromise the progress of the school? In other words, what's their motivation?

Human behavior is functional, contextual, and thoroughly learned. It is heavily influenced by culture, worldview, attitude, genetics, values, experience, and others. Moreover, the habits learned may be either positive or negative, depending on the context. The school member who talks too much in team meetings must have learned he would get his way every time he *railroaded* the conversation. The employee who quit because of a fragile relationship learned the best way to avoid conflict was to turn the other way and run.

Fortunately, behaviors can also be unlearned and habits broken. Through positive intervention, the foundational leader has the responsibility to teach appropriate replacement behaviors. Obviously, this is easier said than done.

Human behavior also has a functional side, stemming from the individual's motivation to gain something or avoid something. For example, staff members may complete their assignment because they want to receive good evaluations or act inappropriately in a meeting in order to hide a problem.

Behaviors are contextual because human beings act differently in different settings. A good example is driving down a highway. Everyone speeds occasionally unless there is a particular stretch of the highway bustling with highway patrol officers. This would be an instance of behavioral change. Staff members exhibit similar change patterns with respect to peers, superiors, and subordinates.

Finally, behavior is very human. In a classroom setting, teachers have the authority to request students to sit quietly and listen to instructions, yet it doesn't mean the students comply. Adults can choose inappropriate behavior as well. Imagine a school meeting being called to order. The leader asks for quiet, but they continue talking. Everyone is human, after all.

NORMS IN SCHOOLS

Behaviors unfolding in schools are called norms. Norms permeate everyone's life in all organizations, cultures, and families. They are often conveyed through nonverbal and verbal behaviors with stories and rituals forming part of the routine.

Norms can make or break a school due to their preponderance in shaping its personality, climate, and ability to avoid conflict. Yet, many traditional school leaders ignore norms on the presumption that each member ought to know beforehand how to behave in the school. This attitude leaves the school vulnerable to unrecognized, nonproductive norms that do nothing to advance shared goals. Without clear "ground rules," no coherent values, beliefs, attitudes, or behaviors are present. Having only implicit norms permits certain patterns of interaction to develop imperceptibly over time.

Explicit norms, on the other hand, are expectations with open recognition and acceptance by the members. By accepting them, the members consciously choose them as guideposts for their treatment of one another, for the decisions they make, and for carrying out their work as a cohesive group. Think back to the three examples. Did guideposts channel everyone toward productive behaviors?

Explicit norms have to be systematically and intentionally developed into a working framework. This framework, on one hand, supports certain kinds of behavior and helps the staff, teams, and school to perform their work unimpeded; on the other hand, it dissuades those behaviors interfering with the school's effectiveness. Therefore, only productive norms promoting healthy behaviors should shape the fundamental values of the school.

By now, the advantages should be obvious. The best norms in schools are productive, up-to-date, approved, known, shared, explicit, and formalized as far as possible (Harvey and Drolet, 2004). One of the difficulties—as well as a source of richness—is the variety of cultures, genders, personalities, values, experiences, and worldviews within which they have to take shape.

Behavior in schools is too multifaceted and time-dependent to leave to the natural evolution of habits and behaviors. Purposeful engagement has to occur all the time if behavior is to improve, keeping in mind the paradoxes and the ongoing cycles of conflict produced by those same paradoxes.

Facilitating change always fails if school members have no inclination to work together. Moreover, unproductive behavior relative to the goal of change creates the well-known dysfunction called *groupthink*, where no one is willing to tackle difficult issues because keeping harmony has become too ingrained in the group. When schools avoid dysfunction and conflict to maintain harmony, they become stagnant and find it difficult to prevail.

In order to manage behavior, the foundational leader engages the whole school in processes to help members close ranks in a way that engenders behaviors that promote trust, respect, inclusiveness, openness, and effective decision-making. School members are allowed to add their individuality to the school. This not only enriches the school, but also makes everyone feel connected and assures buy-in.

This said, both explicit and implicit norms identify the individuals best able to handle conflict and communication in the midst of diversity. When a group member offers suggestions and the implicit group norm dictates *unconstructive* feedback, creative ideas are unlikely to flourish. Productive norms should value everyone's input, and only then should those members who refuse to adhere to them be held accountable for any failure to follow through with their commitments to the group effort.

CONFLICT IN SCHOOLS

Bring two or more staff members together and conflict is sure to arise eventually. It's unavoidable and no group of any shape or size can escape it. When it comes to conflict in schools, two notable extremes are separated by the ideal middle. Figure 4.2 illustrates the *Conflict Continuum in Schools*. One extreme represents schools where staff members are normally reluctant to confront conflict. Instead of actually tackling the issue at hand, their members ignore the problem in the hope of maintaining internal harmony. Sadly this extreme runs rampant throughout schools. Educators tend to steer clear of conflict as much as possible. It is not in their nature. The negative effect produces a static state where ideas cannot flow freely.

The opposite extreme is the school with staff members who are not reluctant to act but their response compounds the conflict. Suppose a difference of opinion exists between two employees. Although struggling to find common ground, they are talking too unprofessionally to be able to cooperate. If the school norms cannot manage their conflict productively, the situation hurts the school.

The top portion of the curve in the figure indicates a school climate where productive norms exist. These explicit, productive norms guide behavior. This is the ideal manner for overcoming conflict in schools. It is important to note this figure does not represent a normative bell curve because the "majority" has not reached the ideal state. To the left and right are those who miss the mark, either unwilling to confront behaviors or confronting them improperly. As school staff is better able to confront conflict effectively, their productivity obviously increases.

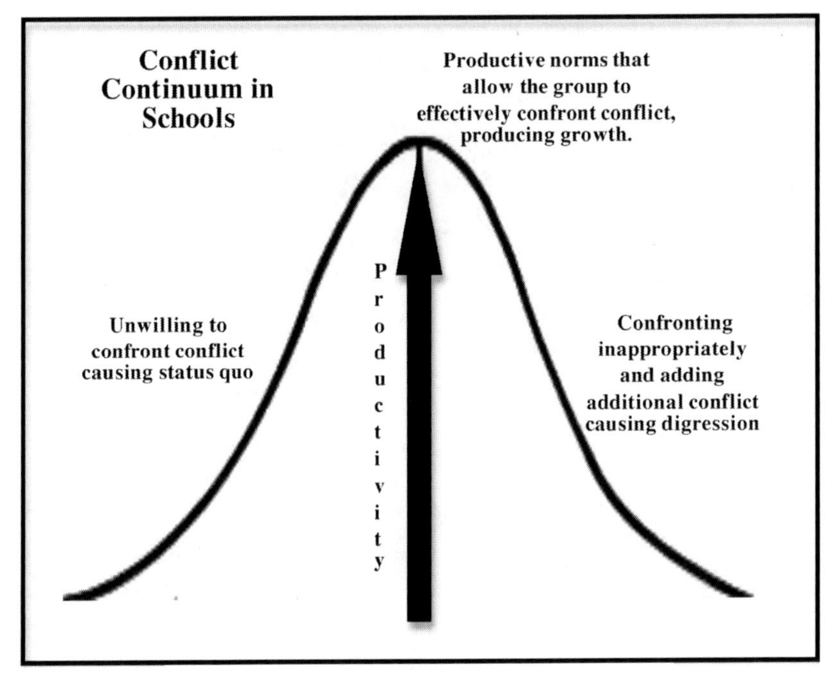

Figure 4.2. Conflict Continuum in Schools

Schools wanting to create a successful, resilient climate, must guide their members to an ideal state. To manage conflict, schools have to initiate, implement, and sustain productive norms. It is the only way to obtain productive results. Failure to do so proactively merely endorses the reigning ineffectiveness.

BUILDING AGREEMENTS: A CYCLICAL PROCESS

The foundational leader tackles the development of productive norms and agreements with the mindset of "Not everyone knows how to behave in a school." The model "Building Agreements: A Cyclical Process" is illustrated in figure 4.3 and serves as a vehicle for the foundational leader to manage behaviors and move the school's capacity to an ideal state on the conflict continuum.

Much of the figure is grounded in the theory of group development proposed by Bruce Tuckman (1965), a renowned American

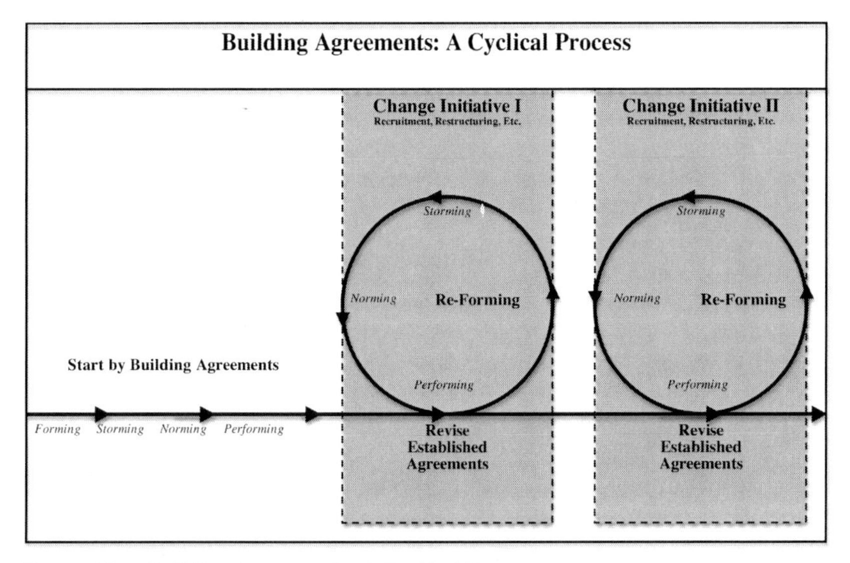

Figure 4.3. Building Agreements: A Cyclical Process

psychologist. Tuckman proposed that groups, as they developed, had to go through a series of pre-defined stages. He called this Forming-Storming-Norming-Performing, and each stage was necessary for growth of any group.

The first stage of "forming" corresponds to group arranging—a type of newness. Here, the group members are positive and courteous. They're busy getting to know one another and sizing up each other's strengths and faults. Some are anxious, while others are excited about the specific task they've been assigned. This is especially prevalent in the opening of a new school or when major restructuring occurs.

When reality sets in, the second stage—"storming"—takes place. This stage exhibits conflict and disagreements among the group members and the leader. Most schools unfortunately are stuck in this stage because the traditional leader often thinks every member is familiar with expected norms. They assume common sense should do the trick. Too bad human behavior doesn't always work out this way. Diversity of opinion or background in schools, for example, can make for some harmful tension. Members are forced to struggle with issues relating to personal versus group identities, perhaps experiencing uncertainty about the direction or purpose of the group. Cliques emerge because some members with common traits are drawn to each other, thereby creating an "us vs. them" mentality. Tension arises.

As uncomfortable as conflict may be, the group, nevertheless, has some maturing to do. Once its members adjust their behaviors to group expectations, the next stage is "norming." Cohesion sets in, and they are able to deal with conflict. They openly share concerns and provide each other with constructive criticism. Relationships effectively turn from competitive to supportive.

At the "performing" stage, the group functions smoothly. It is able to complete tasks because conflict is no longer a barrier. Each member understands his or her role with respect to the group's overall goals. Despite occasional conflict, the group has the capacity to channel energy toward what is positive.

Start by Building Agreements

As denoted in the figure, no matter the school's current stage (forming, storming, norming, or performing), the foremost action is to build consensus by creating meeting designs aimed at the *collective* development of productive norms. By establishing its productive norms, the school acquires the ability to excel during a crucial conflict stage of its development.

Once the productive norms are accepted, everyone has to agree on standard behaviors. Open agreement is critical to the process because it is the leverage for deep change. When someone fails to adhere to the expected behavior he or she *agreed* on, the foundational leader could question the staff member's integrity. Talk about influence.

In addition, everyone agreeing to the norms makes it much easier for staff members to hold one another accountable. In actuality, this is specifically what the foundational leader aims for when building agreements. When all school members–no matter their position–are holding one another accountable for the agreements, the school's culture transforms quickly. Agreements help because, when holding one another accountable, the contracted "rules" take away the subjectivity.

Continuously "Re-Forming" and "Revisiting" Agreements

What sets this model apart from others is the acknowledgement of regression sparked by any type of change effort in schools. Any major transformation—for example, recruitment, restructuring, new systems, or others—has the potential to cause a group to revert to preceding stages of development. Enclosed in the model is a shaded area denoting any type of change initiative. This causes a reversion to an earlier stage and requires everyone to revise the established agreements. Failure to do so causes schoolwide paralysis and an inability to overcome upcoming tensions.

If, for example, a school is operating in the "performing" stage, nearly everyone is working collaboratively and effectively. They have already passed the conflict stage (storming) and established a highly efficient way of doing things together (norming). To no one's surprise, a new school year arrives accompanied by three new staff members. This change in staffing has the potential to spark a relapse when the school moves back to a "forming" stage, which the foundational leader calls "re-forming."

The same is true for any type of enterprise taken on by the school. New systems or procedures compel new dynamics where things are done differently, which compels regrouping, bringing everyone back to square one. To assist the school in progressing through each of the stages (especially storming), the foundational leader brings everyone together to generate and continuously revisit productive, explicit norms. It is a cycle that cannot be ignored.

As the school embarks on any "initiative," it instinctively digresses toward a re-forming stage as the school members try to re-orient themselves to the new task and routine. As outlined in figure 4.2, any change marks an opportune moment for the school members to revisit and perhaps revise previous agreements.

Although the school may have reached the "norming" or "performing" stage, the necessary adaptations could move it back to a more primitive stage of development requiring working with new personnel, systems, or programs. If they do not adapt, the change could force conflicts for which the group is unprepared. The most important thing to avoid is becoming mired in unending conflict.

The cycle of re-forming is never-ending. It happens whenever the experience of change forces the school to revisit or revise its agreements. Given the unavoidability of conflict, the foundational leader takes control by creating a school environment where productive norms are always present. The context of a school is not automatically given and a school's success may hinge on its ability to overcome conflict. How a school elects to act may well create a hospitable, sustaining context or it may create a hostile and adversarial one. A positive context is hardly possible without the vehicle of the school that engenders it.

No doubt bringing all the members of the school together can help achieve a positive context. They can go a long way toward building a sound foundation because they can put effective processes in place to draw the system as a whole into building agreement. With agreement comes the institutionalization of productive norms. This is an ongoing process, which takes persistence, time, and effort, because agreement is constantly changing as the school faces new internal and external challenges of change.

5

METHODS FOR BUILDING PRODUCTIVE NORMS: CREATING COMMON VALUES AND PRINCIPLES

To change a habit, make a conscious decision, then act out the new behavior.

—Maxwell Maltz

Chapter 5 revolves around a short story about a school at one time filled with tension and dysfunction. In the course of building agreements, the school was able to change the harmful behaviors causing utter chaos and dysfunction. Eventually, the school acquired a fresh, new personality, bustling with trust, confidence, and collegiality.

Throughout the story, one can see a host of key elements and techniques employed in the process of building agreements.

AN INTRODUCTION TO AGREEMENTS

The new principal arrived on Monday to be greeted with enthusiasm by the office staff and a handful of teachers. Rumors had already made their way to the school that the new principal valued relationships. She was quite different from the previous principal who operated under a laissez-faire, hands-off leadership style. Because his manner was actually so hands-off, the school was running amok. It seemed as if whenever anyone needed assistance, the principal couldn't be found. And if he were found, his response was typically, "You will need to resolve the issue on your own." No wonder dysfunction was ever so present and out of control.

Over the past few years, the school had significant drops in test scores. Not only was it normal for the staff to speak loudly to the students, it also wasn't unusual for them to criticize one another.

Staff meetings were filled with negativity and lack of enthusiasm. Every initiative the former principal presented was confronted with hostility. His consistent failure to address unprofessional behaviors made the situation awkward. Aggression and resentment were just *the way they did things around there.*

Not many people were happy. Parents, staff, and community members complained to district personnel on a regular basis about the principal losing control. At one board meeting, a group of students, parents, and community members protested the employment of the principal. After a multitude of attempts to have the principal dismissed, the board finally took action.

The new principal had quite a bit of mending fences to do. Going back to the "Conflict Continuum in Schools," this school was nowhere near "ideal." In fact, both extremes were regrettably present—everyone was either unwilling to confront behaviors or confronted them in an unprofessional manner.

The school was unhealthy and needed a boost. Of course, the new principal could have come in "cleaning house," writing up staff members left and right, but she knew they needed much more.

For the first few days, the new principal immersed herself in the school, listening to people and the environment. She sent an electronic survey to the entire staff and determined the informal leaders, which allowed her to begin building alliances with those individuals.

She visited every single classroom, talked with students and parents, and listened to conversations in the lunchroom. In preparation for her first staff meeting, she met with everyone and asked three simple questions:

1. What is working well at the school?
2. What is the one thing you can do to help improve the school?
3. How can I support you in improving that one thing?

There were definitely no secrets. People were more than willing to spill the beans, so to speak.

People and the environment were communicating in harmony. Both messages shrieked loudly, "Help!" Student achievement and staff morale were in the dumps. Everyone wanted to be a part of a successful, resilient school with the capacity to thrive during difficult times.

On Thursday of her second week at the school, the first staff meeting would be held later in the afternoon. In preparation, she had already met with each of the informal leaders to discuss the initiation of productive norms and ways in which they could change the school's climate almost overnight. Consensus indicated the first step was to "re-form" and develop shared values to steer the behaviors of everyone—including the principal.

In preparation, the principal sought an inclusive meeting design to engage everyone in dialogue around desired norms. To assist, she employed the following steps:

1. Everyone was given one index card and placed in groups of six to eight with the chairs arranged in a circular fashion.
2. Everyone was asked to write one desired norm or expectation to create a school culture more conducive to collegiality and group effort.
3. Each group was assigned a recorder to document the sharing of each member's desired norm on a large poster in the middle of the circle. (Note: The principal strategically designated the

informal leaders as the recorders and trained them in ways to initiate deeper dialogue.)

4. After each staff member's statement, the recorder asked the group if they understood the desired norm, agreed with the norm, or had some reservations about the norm.
5. When the group reached consensus about the norm, the recorder left it on the poster and moved to the next person in the group.
6. Everyone continued to share their desired norms until all the cards within the group were read and clarified.
7. Once each group was finished, the meeting transitioned back to whole-staff where each recorder briefly summarized their group's dialogue and posted their respective poster for all to see.

The next step was to winnow down everyone's desired norms to represent the highest leverage norms with ultimately the greatest impact. To do this, the principal facilitated the Spend a Dot technique, as follows:

8. Everyone was given ten colored dots and partnered with another staff member. They were asked to walk around the room (similar to a gallery walk), exchange ideas on the various norms, and vote on the ones they jointly felt would have the maximum influence on building a positive school climate and culture.
9. The principal counted the number of dots for each desired norm, announced that the top fifteen norms would serve as the initial guideposts for accepted behavior, and asked if anyone would have difficulty committing to the newly established norms.

Each person in the room approved the norms and agreed they would fulfill their part in making them a reality. The norms they established were:

- Always show respect for all
- Keep humor and have fun

- Be honest at all times
- Keep an adventurous spirit
- Always share and be open
- Focus on solutions rather than problems
- Always value the ideas of others
- Don't take things personally
- Always stay open to suggestions
- Act as a united front
- Always listen actively
- Continuously build trust

These productive norms were posted throughout the school and discussed at the beginning of every staff meeting. Not only were the agreements talked about during staff meetings, the principal also encouraged members to make any necessary additions or alterations as needed. For the next couple of months, the school was on the right track. Everyone kept personal agendas on the back burner, while following the agreed upon norms when working together.

The school was in an upswing. For the most part, the school was transitioning to the "performing" stage, as everyone was able to participate in healthy discussions and disagreements.

Is It Time to Regroup?

After another month, the school was healthier than it had been in recent years. Although the principal had to rein in a couple of teachers to remind them of the agreed upon behaviors, the majority were working diligently in the follow-through of those expectations.

The principal continued to "listen" and pay attention to her surroundings. In fact, some interesting data emerged. The scores from grade-level common assessments and district benchmarks (paying attention to the environment), along with guidance from the leadership team (listening to people), demonstrated a need for change.

In response, the principal instituted a new system, requiring teachers to analyze common assessments on a bi-weekly basis and to move students based on the results of those assessments. One staff member would re-teach the students who did not score at grade level, while the other would offer enrichment to those meeting grade-level standards. This new system demanded teachers assigning their students to other teachers based on the needs of the student. This was much easier said than done.

One teacher stated, "You mean I have to take some students not even officially assigned to me?"

Another argued, "I am held accountable for my students' test scores. I am not too sure if I feel comfortable letting someone else teach them."

The principal responded, "Remember our agreements. We all concurred we would 'Stay flexible' and 'Value one another's strengths.'"

Yet, there was still a look of discomfort on everyone's faces. They were scared. After so many years of an ingrained culture of teacher isolation, this was taking the act of "working together" to another level. This was a major change initiative and the principal recognized a fitting time to "re-form" and to revisit the existing agreements.

She knew if the school plowed forward without attending to the established agreements, they would take one step forward and two steps back.

In reality, the principal knew this time was inevitable because the opening agreements were so general. They needed much more clarification and much deeper dialogue. Thus, the principal employed another set of activities.

Finding Themes

It was apparent to the principal and leadership team that the existing agreements needed some clearing up. They examined each agreement and categorized them into four distinct categories as displayed in figure 5.1, *Existing Agreements Themed.* They included:

1. Open Lines of Communication
2. Valuing the Strengths of Others
3. Creating a "Village" Mentality
4. Excitement in the Workplace.

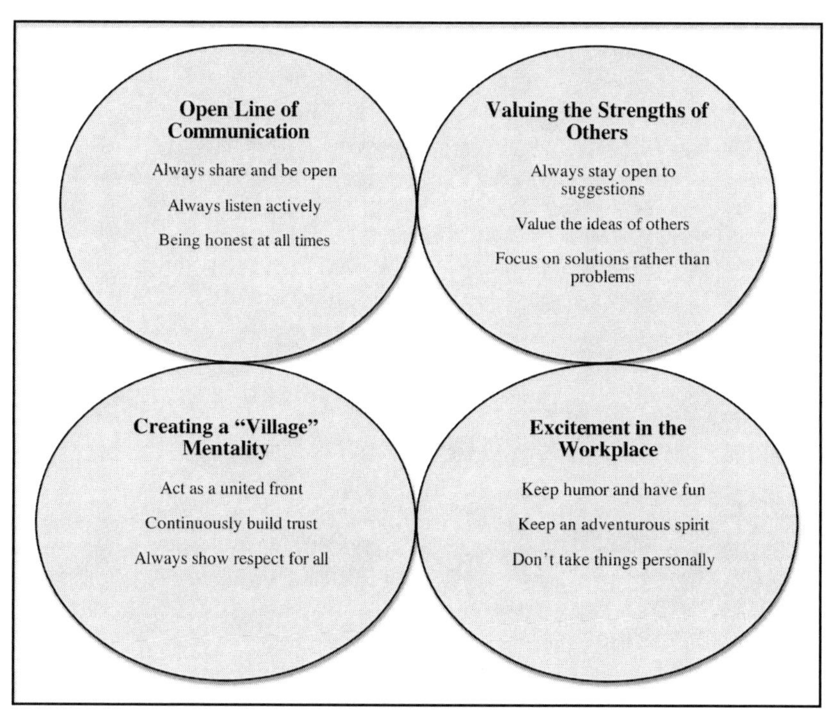

Figure 5.1. Existing Agreements Themed

"We are seeing themes. What comes next?" the principal asked the leadership team, which created a short pause as everyone stared at each other. The principal drew from her extensive toolbox of "listening" techniques and had everyone participate in the Strengths, Weaknesses, Opportunities, and Threats (S.W.O.T.s) activity to spur additional dialogue and generate new ideas. Although the existing agreements spawned an abundance of "strengths" and "opportunities," a select few "weaknesses" and "threats" stood out like sore thumbs.

"Ah ha," thought the principal, "The existing agreements are too general." They needed further refinement to more specific behaviors. For example, what did "Always share and be open" look like in the day-to-day dealings of the staff? When tensions arose, the staff needed a specific strategy. With the upcoming assessment initiative with teachers informally sharing students, there was a need for the school to concentrate solely on creating an "open line of communication."

There it was, right in front of their faces.

"Let's develop some vital behaviors to polish each of the agreements within the area of open line of communication."

It Takes Vital Procedures

The principal knew certain staff members would not feel comfortable unofficially handing over their students to colleagues without an open line of communication. Trust, respect, and relationships had to prevail and everyone had to follow suit.

The principal designed a meeting for the staff to expand the agreements encased in the area of open line of communication and to develop school-wide communication. The communication agreements consisted of:

1. Always share and be open.
2. Always listen actively.
3. Be honest at all times.

The question at hand now was: What *specific actions* must everyone contribute in order to carry out those agreements? In other words, what vital behaviors were needed to develop everyone's ability to communicate effectively with one another—ultimately improving trust and interpersonal relationships?

"Listening" to Generate New Ideas

Some initial thought had to surface before the staff had the necessary tools to answer the question. To provoke forethought on the topic, the principal developed an online survey called Vital Procedures Survey, which contained only three questions. The information gathered from each question would serve as a springboard for determining "specific actions" needed to improve communication. Figure 5.2, Vital Procedures Survey, illustrates each of the three survey questions.

1. Honesty - How do you want yourself and others to exemplify honesty?

Example: I want people to feel that if they have a question or concern, they can approach me and be honest with their feelings. I also want to ensure I am honest with myself as I self-reflect on my leadership practices.

2. Ability to Share and Be Open - How do you want yourself and others to exemplify the ability to share and be open?

Example: When I have a misunderstanding or question about something that someone is doing or saying, I want to first "master my stories." This means that I do not want to make up stories in my own head that may not be true as to the reasoning behind their behaviors or actions. Next, I want to talk to the individual to clarify the misunderstanding--instead of speaking to others, which may lead to rumors.

3. Active Listening - How do you want yourself and others to exemplify active listening?

Example: When I am having a conversation with another staff member, it is important that both of us demonstrate good listening skills, such as paraphrasing, asking clarifying questions, mirroring body language, and making eye contact.

Figure 5.2. Vital Procedures Survey

As one can see, the first question on the survey asked, "How do you want yourself and others to exemplify honesty?" Each staff member could reflect on the "specific actions" others could put into practice–leading to honesty between colleagues.

The thought-provoking survey produced useful data for an upcoming meeting the principal planned. A handful of responses included:

- "I want to feel I can express myself without judging others . . . in this way I will help other people feel safe."
- "If a staff member has a concern regarding any given issue, I would appreciate if he or she came directly to me and informed me of their feelings instead of going around other staff members and telling them how they feel about the way I handle such situations. I believe it is much more productive if I am aware of how others feel and perceive me so I can do something about it, change it, fix it, or whatever necessary. If I am not aware, I cannot do anything about it."

- "I am able to share and be open because I will demonstrate kindness and empathy in all situations and be solution driven as opposed to gossiping or dwelling on issues."
- "Speak with a calm tone, and get to the point. No dwelling on the situation and the 'buts', 'what if's', and excuses."
- "I like for people to make eye contact and ask questions if they have not understood. The questions that help my thinking are clarifying questions that ask for specific and concrete examples."
- "Two-way conversation is important. Sometimes one tends to be the talker most of the time, and the other person just stands there and listens or tries to listen when in fact they have something to say, but the other person does not allow that to happen as they like to be the center of the conversation. Be fair in talking to others—listen too."

Once the information was gathered, it was time to "re-form" and attend to the continuous cycle of building agreements.

RE-FORMING AND BUILDING AGREEMENTS AGAIN

The meeting agenda was set and the principal was eager to see the outcome. Everyone walked in for the meeting to see the seats arranged in three large circles. At the center of each circle were two large posters: one had the three existing communication agreements, while the other contained only the words, "Vital Procedures."

Prior to the meeting, each staff member received a document containing the staff responses from the Vital Procedures Survey. They were asked to look through each set of responses to see if anything jumped out.

Once everyone was seated, the meeting began. The principal began by introducing the agenda and the expected outcome: The staff would work together to create and come to an agreement on the vital behaviors for maintaining open lines of communication.

After introducing the upcoming course of action, the meeting was set in motion.

1. Each of the three groups were seated in their respective circle and given twenty minutes to discuss only one vital procedure for their specific agreement. For example, one group attended to "Always share and be open," while another group discussed "Always listen actively." To help with the process, each group had the survey data readily available.
2. Once the groups completed their one vital procedure, a member from each group shared the procedure with the whole staff—spurring deep follow-up questions and clarification.
3. Next, each of the agreement and procedure posters was rotated to a different group. Each group again had the charge of developing an additional vital procedure for the new agreement, followed by another sharing session.
4. Rotations occurred a third time to ensure each group had input on the development of a vital procedure for each of the three agreements.
5. The last step involved group discussion and agreement on the vital procedures.

Not only did the process advance the initial agreements, it also spurred deep, meaningful conversation. Many staff members stepped out of their comfort zone and shared the specifics of how they want to be treated.

It is important to note that, as the staff agreed on the new procedures, there were instances when they didn't have the answers. When these instances occurred, everyone looked to the principal pleading, "Help us out here." In response, the principal kept quiet, looking at each member and sending the message: *These aren't my agreements—they're yours.*

Once an agreement was established, the new vital procedures (fig. 5.3) materialized. The principal knew this was only the beginning. There were other areas still needing attention, along with

The Ability to Share and Be Open

Vital Procedure #1:

Focus on the message, not the messenger.

Vital Procedure #2:

Communicate and touch base regularly.

Vital Procedure #3:

Respecting and observing professional social norms

Always Listening Actively

Vital Procedure #1:

Focus on the message, not the messenger.

Vital Procedure #2:

Communicate and touch base regularly.

Vital Procedure #3:

Respecting and observing professional social norms

Being Honest at all Times

Vital Procedure #1:

Focus on the message, not the messenger.

Vital Procedure #2:

Communicate and touch base regularly.

Vital Procedure #3:

Always respect the professional social norms.

Figure 5.3. Vital Procedures

other initiatives that would develop throughout each school year. In order to continue moving toward the building of a successful, resilient school, everyone must continuously engage in the foundation of building agreements.

The school had a successful year. Their assessment system blossomed and became a model for the district. Relationships flourished and, most importantly, students learned, as evidenced by a spike in test scores.

RAVINES, GULLIES, AND CANYONS

It is never too late for the foundational leader to begin changing behaviors. Look at the previous story. The school was operating at the bottom of the barrel, yet through the continuous cycle of building agreements, they were able to prevail.

It takes time—many types of behavior are developed incrementally over years—but all behavior can be modified.

Habit-forming behaviors inside schools can be compared to the ravines, gullies, and canyons caused by water erosion. Many have seen the water flow through small, shallow impressions caused in the earth or in gullies through which someone can drive a large car. Or, most spectacular of all, the Grand Canyon. Geologists speculate the Grand Canyon was carved out over millions of years by melted snow and ice, producing torrents of water.

Habits are much the same; they become deeper and more ingrained over time. If unconstructive, they can erode otherwise vibrant schools. Some harmful behaviors may only be small rifts, which are relatively easy to fix; others become deep ravines, which can be a real headache to fix. The more ingrained the habits, the harder they are to modify. There is no alternative because, left unattended, they are liable to develop into canyons.

Repairing the erosion with positive behaviors takes time and incremental steps born of patience.

6

FOUNDATION #3: CO-CREATING PURPOSE

Many organizations have little sense of purpose beyond their own sense of organization.

—Unknown

Under traditional leadership, small groups become notoriously hopeless at developing their own goals, mission, or visions. Co-creating purpose, the foundation discussed in this chapter, is about combining a clear, compelling school vision with values rooted in everyone's personal ideals and aspirations. It's about purpose, strategically formed through sustained dialogue among the members of a school and the development of shared goals.

The foundational leader seeks a coherent narrative from a host of individual experiences, worldviews, and perceptions by bringing together as many school members as possible. Within this narrative, the values and goals of all the players coalesce into a single set of themes and meanings. Regardless of the circumstances, the project

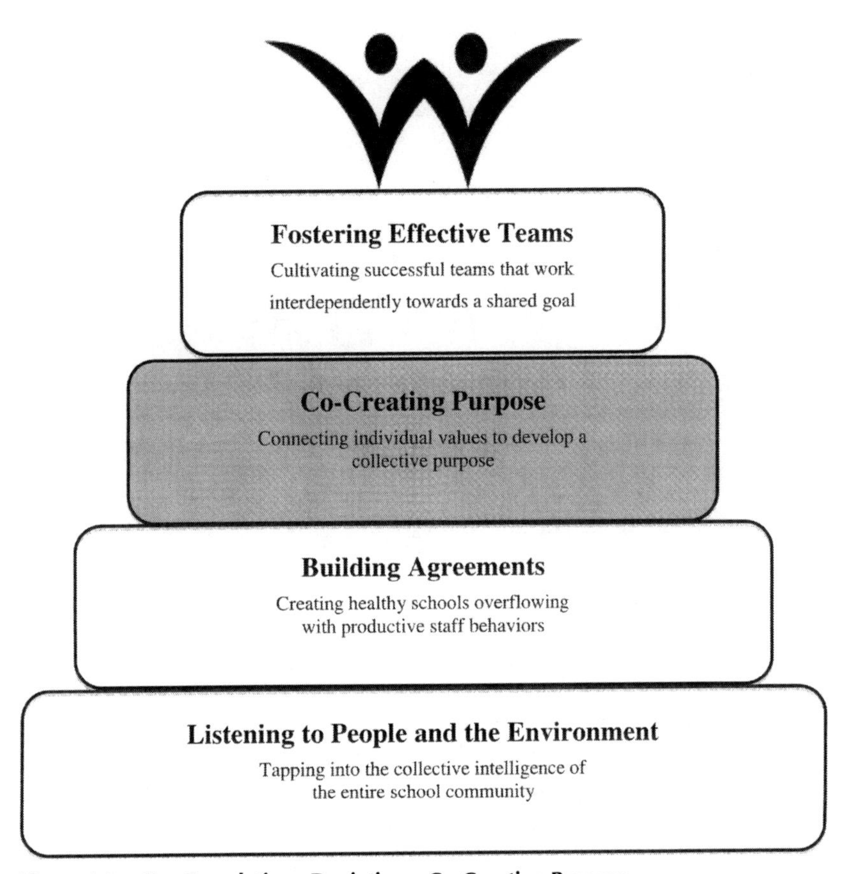

Figure 6.1. Key Foundations Depiction—Co-Creating Purpose

of co-creating purpose must take place in an open exchange of ideas; in other words, the dialogue has to be authentic.

This chapter offers a step-by-step model for the foundational leader to provide an inclusive environment where individuals are free to share their personal views and ambitions. Such an environment inspires enthusiasm and passion. Participation drives people to make processes more effective and to be unselfish in their commitments.

THE CHALLENGES OF BUILDING PURPOSE

Collective purpose takes time and cannot be created overnight. As delineated in the second foundation, building agreements, productive norms are a precursor to an open, honest climate where school members can begin to explore individual and school values, beliefs, and goals. However, purpose requires strategic initiatives to take dialogue to a higher plane for the individual and joint goals of stakeholders rather than shelving output in the hope of revisiting it sometime later.

If they operate with little sense of purpose, schools fall victim to a variety of dysfunctions, ranging from employee dissatisfaction and low morale to low productivity and burnout. Combined with current realities, any of these afflictions can make a disagreeable climate.

By contrast, schools with a strong sense of joint purpose have the wherewithal to create healthy environments to empower the members. Purposeful schools cultivate forward-looking and motivated individuals, and the collective plots the changes necessary to create resilient schools. As Warren Bennis and Burt Nanus (2005) pointed out:

> When the organization has a clear sense of its purpose, direction, and desired future state and when this image is widely shared, individuals are able to find their roles both in the organization and in the larger society of which they are a part. This empowers individuals and confers status upon them because they can see themselves as a part of a worthwhile enterprise. They gain a sense of importance, as they are transformed from robots blindly following instructions to human beings engaged in a creative purposeful venture. (53–84)

Although it takes time and patience to form an enterprise worth fighting for, one step at a time should do it. It is of utmost importance for everyone to be open and honest; however, some school members may feel safer under the cloak of confidentiality. Any request for confidentiality must be taken seriously, especially if the dialogue is not yet completely open and honest. In the end, diversity of views must not be devalued, and the members have to master the skills of both listening and self-expression.

The creation of purpose is not the job of the leader only. The foundational leader understands everyone has to participate in order to form a shared vision—that is, the collective picture of what everyone desires for the school. The big picture has to issue forth from within each person who will have a starring role before purpose becomes truly shared and evident to everyone.

CO-CREATING PURPOSE: A STEP-BY-STEP PROCESS

The step-by-step model (fig. 6.2) in this chapter rests on the idea: "to co-create means to form together." In order to co-create, the school has to tap the reservoir of personal and professional purposes its members are encouraged to divulge. Without individual purpose, its collective vision has no substance.

Two strong motivations are at work here. On one hand, the members value their private and broad professional purposes as their own, and are unwilling to give them up. On the other hand, the school has to weave those purposes into a single cultural narrative. A *we*-culture takes hold only when people find meaning in their present careers and their lives. Their combined values, goals, and visions represent not merely diversity, they represent unstoppable progress for the school. For the purpose to emerge naturally, the needs of each side have to be satisfied.

Three steps support the emergence of collective purpose. The first step encourages members to explore their personal purposes. The second recognizes common themes, goals, and values among the members. Third, the school has to encapsulate those relationships into a single overarching purpose.

Step 1: Support Individual Purpose

Individuality infuses authenticity into personal pursuit, inviting an ongoing effort to find meaning in professional life. The first step in co-creating purpose involves the personal goals and values of the employee. A circle (fig. 6.3) can represent an individual's sense of purpose in the school. Inside the circle are his or her personal values, vision, and goals.

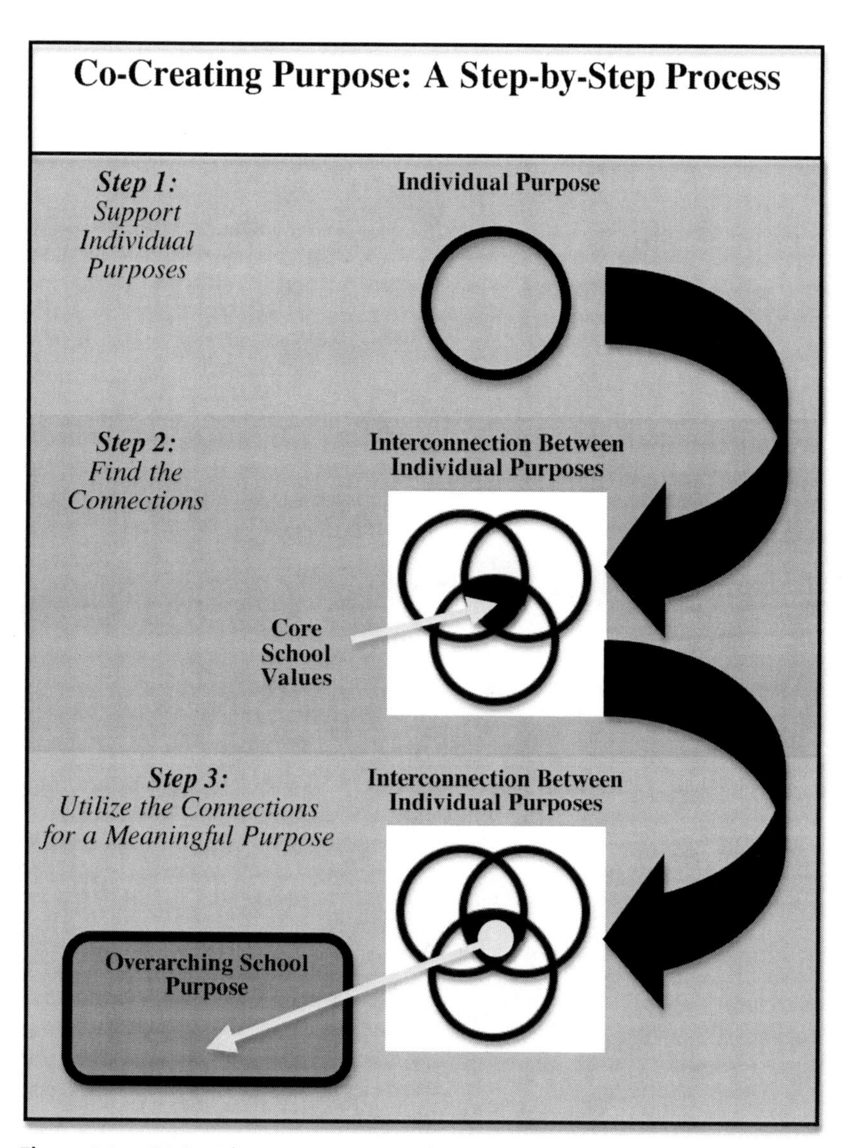

Figure 6.2. Co-Creating Purpose: A Step-by-Step Process

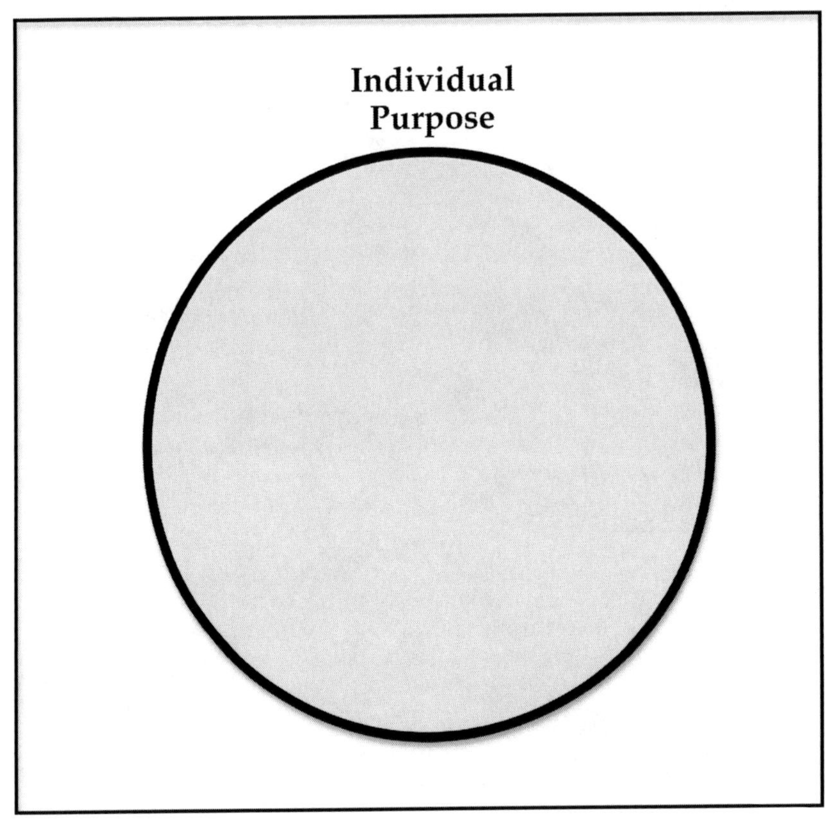

Figure 6.3. Circle Representing Individual Purpose

Some staff members spend too much time on the job, leading to burnout and dissatisfaction. Others plod on, detached in relation to their professional obligations, preferring to spend most of their working hours thinking about personal matters. When members struggle to balance their personal and professional lives, they bring a measure of dysfunction to the school.

As a "system thinker," the foundational leader forms a holistic purpose by affording school members regular opportunities to explore their individual purposes. It is preferable to have a member who lives a purposeful, driven life than one who does not. Foundational leaders want school members to discover their life purposes. They want them to wake up each morning excited about the challenges of the day. The opposite—school members waking up dreading the day's challenges, having no real purpose in life, and living like robots—leave the school at a disadvantage. It's just plain common sense.

At times, the foundational leader has to act as a counselor or therapist for each member of the school. Relationships on such a "personal" level lie within the scope of their responsibilities because individual purpose is a stepping-stone toward the collective purpose every foundational leader seeks for the school.

The foundational leader searches below the surface in order to enliven work attitudes continually through purpose. This leader knows a lack of individual purpose is a call for concern, and timely action can create new opportunities to recover lost meaning. Inaction in the face of a school member's discontent ultimately diminishes the effectiveness of the school. As soon as the leader expresses interest in the ways employees view their purpose, a perceptible shift emerges. Suddenly, the school members feel more valued and respected.

Abraham Maslow's (1943) hierarchy of needs (fig. 6.4) may come in handy as the foundational leader strives to spark dialogue on the goals and values of life. Maslow argued that human motivation surrounds five levels of human needs, including physiological, safety, love and belonging, esteem, and self-actualization. When needs at one level are met, individuals were more apt to experience the next level of personal growth until they realized their fullest potential, or self-actualization.

School members feel anxiety and tension at every level of this hierarchy. When facilitating and empowering them to find personal purpose, every good leader should be mindful of that anxiety. After all, facilitating a process is meaningful only when it takes account of the living human being, not an abstraction.

The foremost needs are the obvious requirements for human survival—physiological needs. These include food, water, sleep, and others. If, for instance, a staff member were struggling with personal finances—leading to stress and chronic sleep deprivation—the particular individual would not operate to his or her fullest potential, which, in turn, has harmful effects on the school.

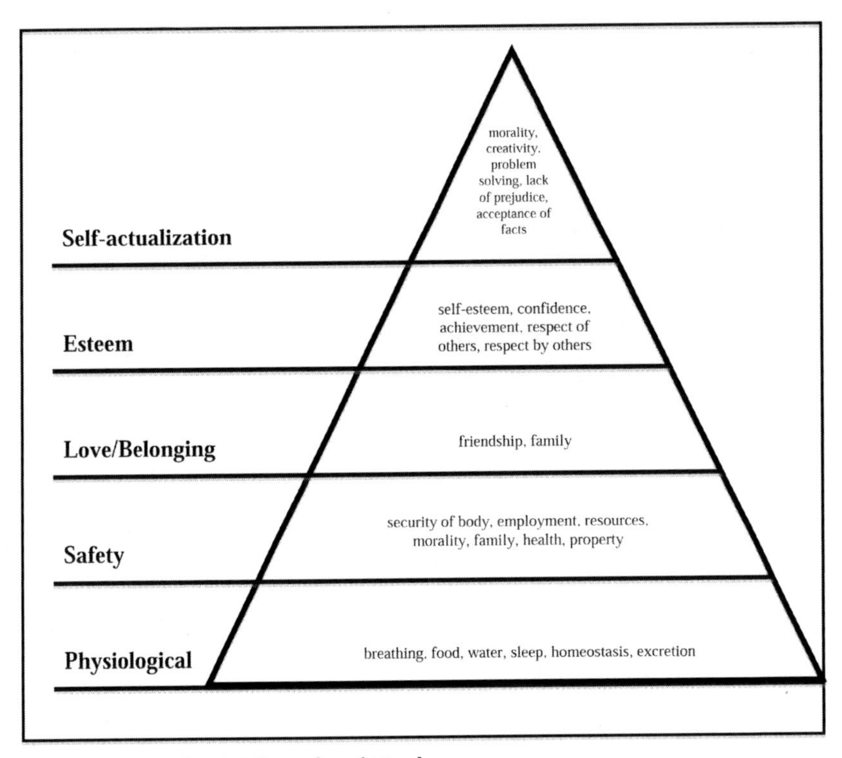

Figure 6.4. Maslow's Hierarchy of Needs

Safety was the second level in Maslow's model. This notion stresses individual need for predictability. People want to feel safe and secure whether it comes from personal and financial security or health and well-being. The third level of human needs, Love/Belonging, was social. Individuals have a strong need to feel a sense of belonging and acceptance from the groups to which they belong. In the case of a school, each member yearns to be respected and valued, as both an individual and a contributing member to the school as a whole.

Following the feeling of acceptance, people develop self-esteem and confidence. Those who achieve the human need for self-respect improve their self-image and accept themselves internally. Self-actualization, the last level, can occur only when each preceding level has been attained. This final stage of psychological development is when an individual realizes his or her full potential. Self-actualization spurs determination and aspirations for something bigger—personal purpose.

Both positive and negative experiences help us recognize meaning in our lives. A foundational leader listens and understands where all members are "coming from," where they are presently, and where they want to go. They may desire the same direction as everyone else in the school, or they may choose a different path. The foundational leader encourages them to discover their passions, goals, and values.

Step 2: Find the Connections

With the preliminary stage of dialogue out of the way, it's time to connect the discovered values and meanings. If your school consists of eighty staff members, it is common knowledge that eighty private purposes relate to the overriding purpose of the school as a whole.

Consider four circles (fig. 6.5). Each circle represents each member's life purposes; however, each individual purpose is separate from the other. On the surface, there may be no common features.

Remember, nothing is wrong with diversity. Activities connecting individual vision-oriented purposes should lead to a set of core values, which the school adopts. Figure 6.6 represents the links to each other and the core values of the school.

By taking the time to listen and to value each staff member's dreams and aspirations, the foundational leader can tap into some powerful passions in both their personal and their professional lives. Balancing (or separating) work in relation to private life is important at one level but work often spills into private life and vice versa. They are both too important to keep in separate, sanitized compartments. When one is successful at work, one is happier at home. When blessed with a healthy personal life, mental equilibrium influences performance at work.

In a group, without violating anyone's right to privacy, each member can analyze his or her individual purposes and discern common themes. Their values, beliefs, goals, and aspirations may not be identical, but they are *connected.* After all, who prefers unsuccessful relationships, careers, or personal lives? Who doesn't want

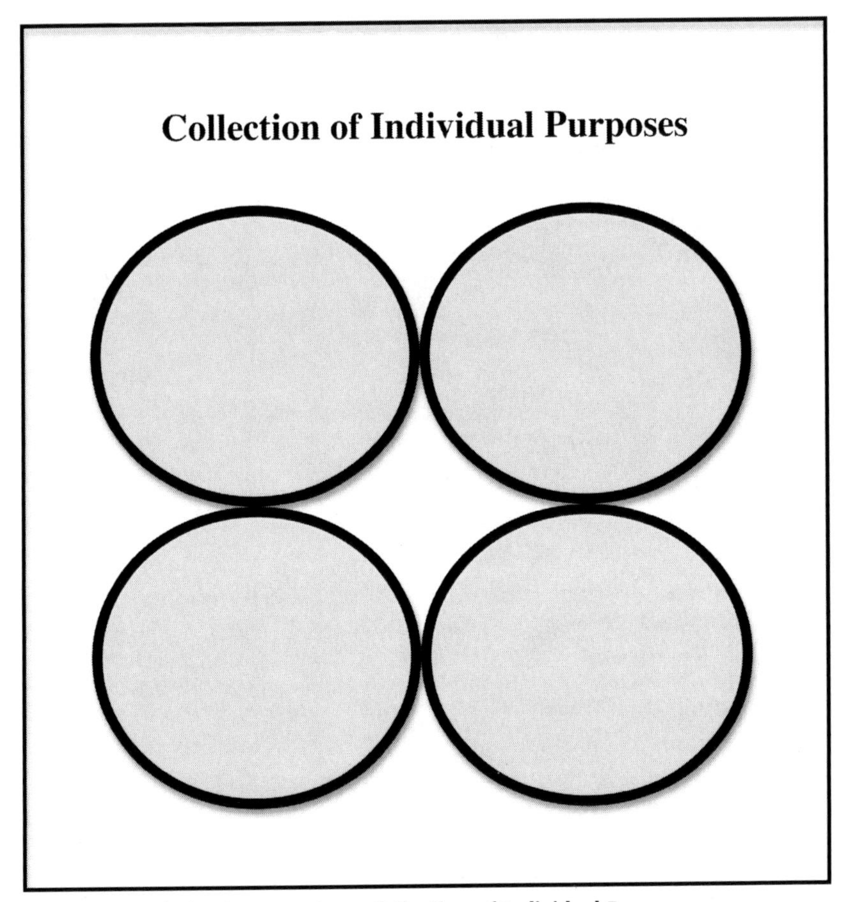

Figure 6.5. Circles Representing a Collection of Individual Purposes

to live a long, healthy life? Once the connections become known, everyone can embark on a collaborative effort to build a tangible school vision and mission.

At that point, the foundational leader can tap into their hearts and ask, "Where do we want to be in a year, or in five or ten years? How are we going to get there?"

Step 3: Use Connections for a Meaningful Purpose

Developing or re-inventing school values, beliefs, and goals are tantamount to changing the culture. If school members contribute a

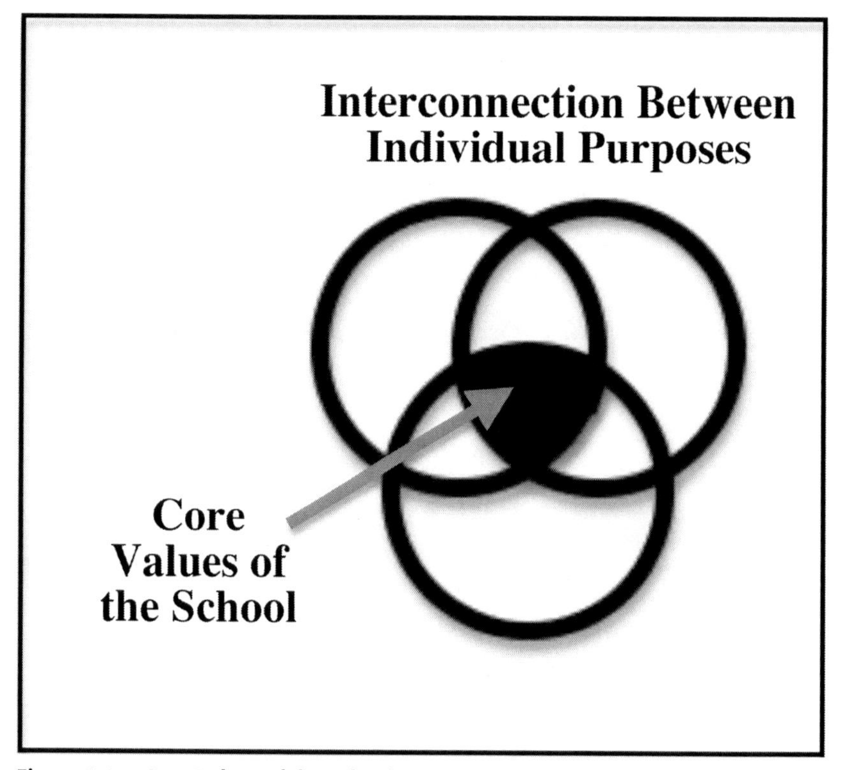

Figure 6.6. Core Values of the School

piece of themselves to this cultural shift, they will be more committed to seeing the planned changes become reality. As stakeholders, they have the right to a meaningful professional life as well as a personal life. They should be able to contribute to the school purpose and become one with the school.

The illustration in figure 6.7 represents the overarching school purpose from the connections between each staff member's individual purposes. The development of purpose through the vision and mission statements serves as a compass for the school and outlines the significant values adopted. A slew of practical large-group processes may be employed in the search for meaning (some explained in the next chapter). In all this, however, the *process* of bringing school members together to co-create purpose is much more valuable than the eloquence of a vision and mission statement on a piece of paper.

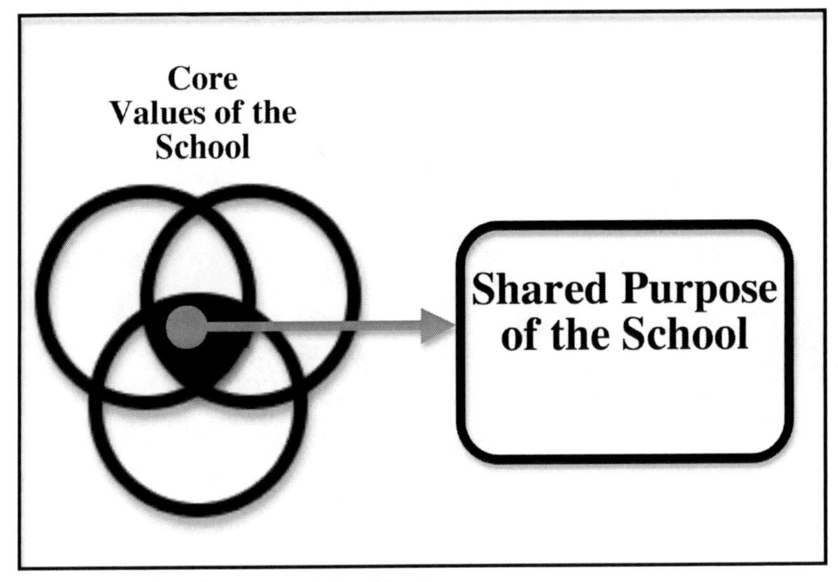

Figure 6.7. Shared Purpose of the School

The foundational leader keeps others enthusiastic, passionate, and moving toward a common goal by co-creating purpose through inclusive dialogue. This maintains focus and discourages wandering aimlessly, or perhaps sleepwalking, through each school year.

7

METHODS FOR CREATING A UNITED PURPOSE: ENGAGING EVERYONE IN DEEP DIALOGUE

No one can force change on anyone else. It has to be experienced. Unless we invent ways where paradigm shifts can be experienced by large numbers of people, then change will remain a myth.

—Eric Trist

Finding shared purpose is no easy task, yet it is critical in the school improvement process. Every school has a distinct culture and climate that set the tone. This has a dramatic effect on everything that happens. When a visitor walks into a school where collaboration is the norm, the staff is visibly open, inclusive, and working well together. On the other hand, when the school is one of negativity and isolation, the staff is disjointed, impatient, and unhappy.

How does the leader successfully change such a complex, deeply ingrained, and toxic culture?

Co-creating purpose achieves change. Of course, a dramatic vision and mission are necessary, but what matters most is the process of getting to collective purpose. Shared ideals embody a profound power of promise to take any school to new heights. When present, school members take on new challenges with enthusiasm and passion because they believe: *It is not all about me anymore. It is about us.*

Included in this chapter is an example of how a new school co-created purpose by bringing together the entire school community. Following the example are two processes (Future Search and The World Café) the foundational leader has in his or her arsenal of techniques for co-creating purpose.

EXAMPLE OF CO-CREATING PURPOSE

The following example shows the development of a vision statement at a new school. It illustrates the step-by-step process of co-creating purpose and clarifies ways in which individual purposes are transformed into a shared sense of purpose.

The school's first task was to invite all the stakeholders to begin exploring their personal values and beliefs. To accomplish this, the school sent an open-ended questionnaire to all members of the school community (parents, students, staff, business owners, and prominent local leaders), approximately 800 persons, from every walk of life.

The questionnaire had one request: "Share in detail a memorable personal experience you had when a parent, student, or staff member from a particular school exceeded your expectations. What did you value about the experience? How did it make you feel?" Hundreds of questionnaires were returned, making up a vast collection of individual purposes.

The next step was to identify the commonalities and interconnections binding the values and beliefs expressed in the responses. To do so, the school invited participants to an event focused on identifying and tapping into the ideals that emerged from the questionnaire.

About 600 people took part in the event. Each of the groups of twenty to twenty-five individuals was assigned a staff member

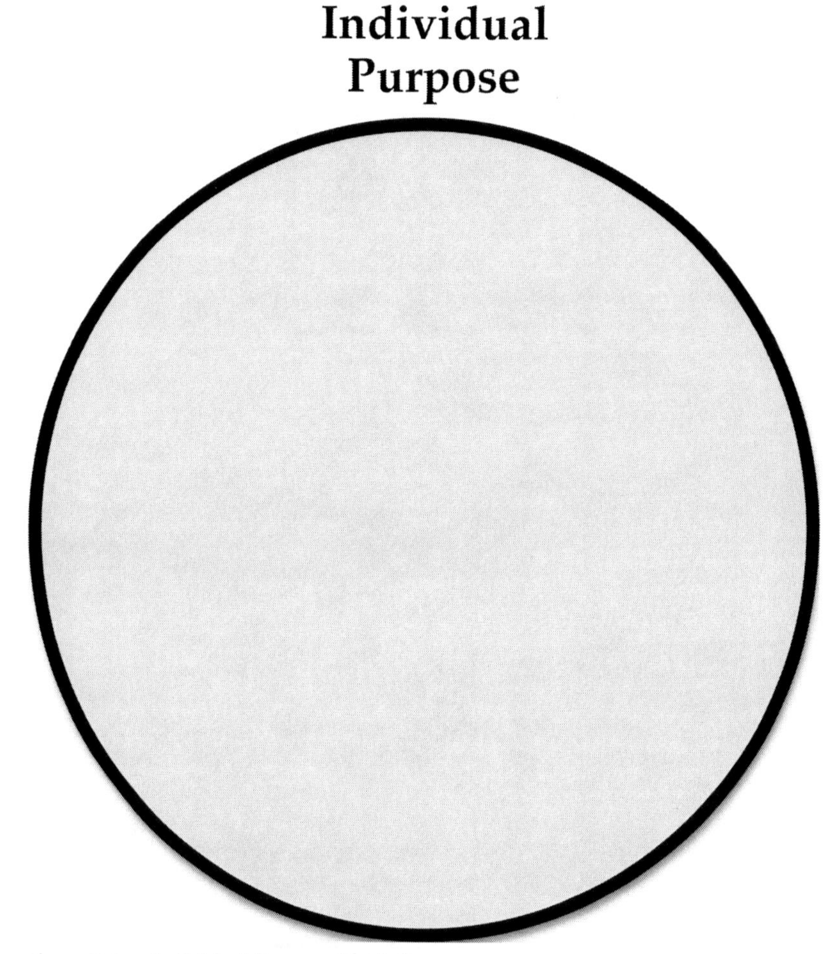

Figure 7.1. Individual Purpose Depiction

charged with facilitating discussion. Of course, the school leader trained those staff members in the specific process of facilitation.

The objective for each group was to present their own questionnaire responses and work out a specific statement encapsulating the group's collective values. Each group was asked to create its own values statement, which would later be linked to the others to design a vision statement.

The entire gathering came together to read the group statements. As the participants presented their results, they commented that

Collection of Individual Purposes

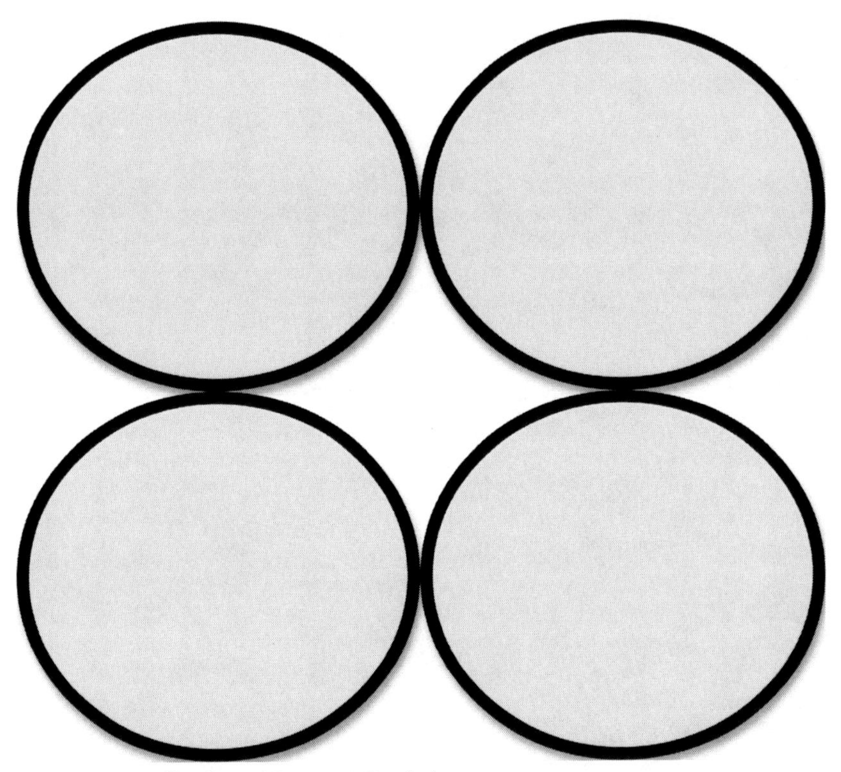

Figure 7.2. Collection of Purposes Depiction

they enjoyed the process of moving their own values and beliefs into one shared statement. Many expressed gratitude for being considered. The opportunity to give their input on the development of the school's purpose, they said, made them feel valued.

Figure 7.5 outlines a handful of the "value statements" collected from this gathering.

Following each group presentation, the school leader pointed to each of the values statements posted throughout the auditorium, and asked excitedly, "Who wants to be a part of a school with these values?" The place erupted with indescribable energy.

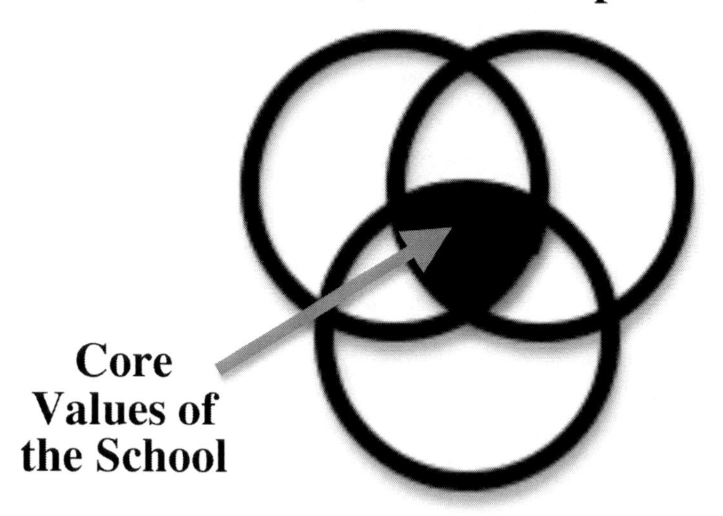

Figure 7.3. Core Values Depiction

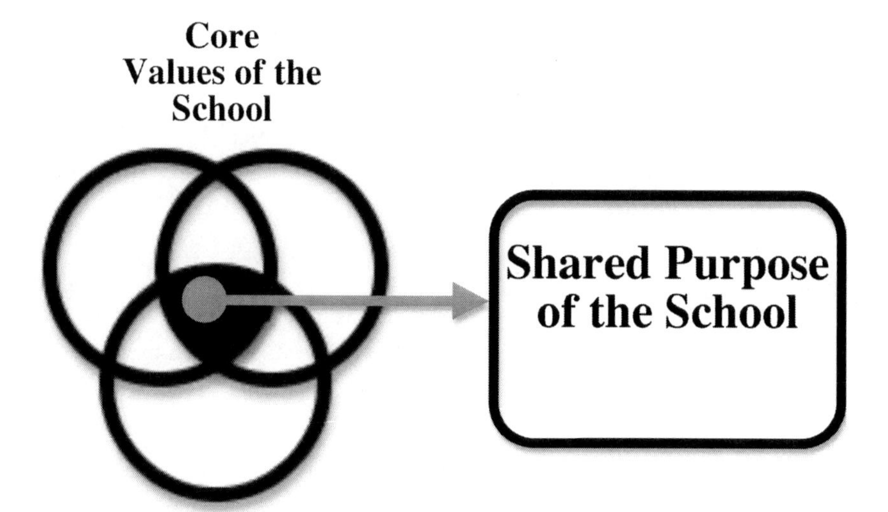

Figure 7.4. Shared Purpose Depiction

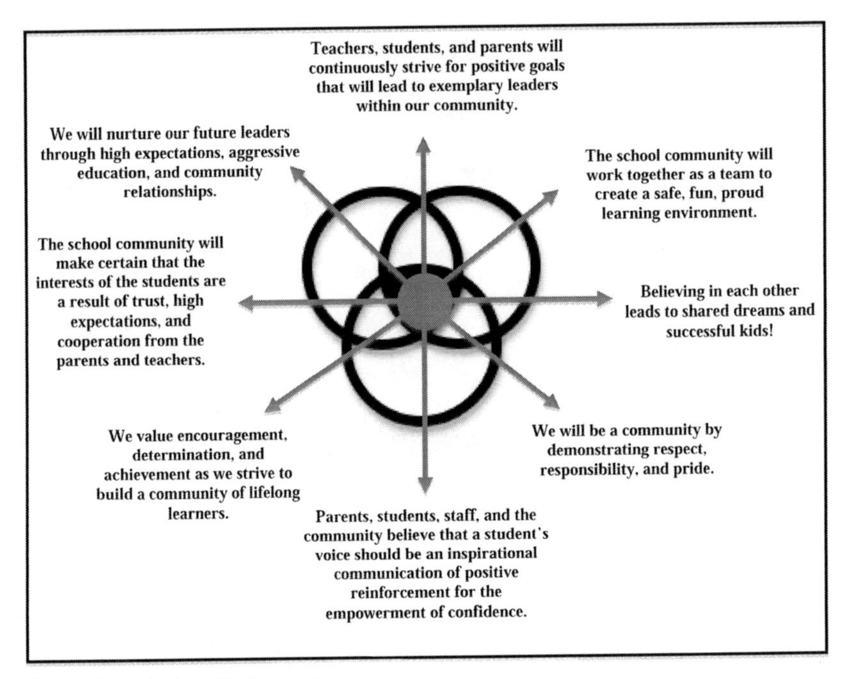

Figure 7.5. Values Statements

One final step remained. The school had yet to construct a meaningful school vision or overarching school purpose based on each of the Values Statements collected, along with the personal values of the school staff.

Since this task took place after the gathering, the school staff (teachers, secretaries, custodians, counselors, and others) was invited to a general meeting. Their participation in a number of processes spurred a dialogue about their own personal beliefs and ideals.

Several meaningful activities later, the staff accepted the following vision statement: "Our vision is to come together with a unified purpose and a passion for nurturing partnerships. Success will be built upon a commitment to teaching through multiple intelligences and growing within learning communities. As a result, we will cultivate a fully integrated school dedicated to high expectations, appreciation of diversity, positive relationships, and a desire for learning."

This is just one quick and easy example of moving from an individual to a collective or joint purpose. Although reaching a final vision statement is valuable, the process of getting to the statement is equally—if not more—significant.

Had a select few been simply brought in to cobble together a vision statement, the other members of the school and its community might not have attached as much meaning to the statement. Instead, everyone had a part in the vision, contributing his or her personal values.

Far from being the end of the journey, a vision statement is merely words on paper . . . unless people step forward to make it a reality. It is revisited often, refined, and included in discussion throughout the school and the community.

A shared purpose guides school members toward making a dream a reality.

FUTURE SEARCH MEETING DESIGN

The process of Future Search enables groups of diverse people to focus on the future and seek common ground. It is appropriate in school settings where the aim is to develop a shared purpose supported by everyone. In a future search, people have a chance to take ownership of their past, present, and future; confirm their mutual values; and commit to action plans grounded in reality (Weisbord and Janoff, 1995).

This commitment-building meeting design typically involves sixty to eighty participants and takes three days. Future search is not a one-time meeting designed to be completed during a typical one to two hour staff meeting. In schools, this may take shape in the form of a retreat during summer break or during off-track time in year-round schools.

The three-day event includes five distinct tasks, including:

1. Review the Past
2. Explore the Present

3. Create Ideal Future Scenarios
4. Identify Common Ground
5. Make Action Plans

Marvin Ross Weisbord and Sandra Janoff (1995) argued that Future Search facilitators should keep the following set of principles in mind when planning:

- Have the right people in the room, including a cross section of the whole or those with authority, resources, information, expertise, and need.
- Create conditions where participants experience the whole "elephant" before acting on any part of it.
- Focus on the future and seek common ground.
- Enable people to take responsibility for their own learning and action plans.

A typical future search agenda begins in the afternoon of the first day and ends the morning of the third day. The authors offered a variety of activities for each of the days.

Day 1—Afternoon: Focus on Past and Focus on Present, External Trends

The first day spans four to five hours. Everyone is working in mixed groups on the first task, focus on the past. They are charged with engaging in deep dialogue and reminiscing about their past personal, global—and school highlights from the past five to ten years.

As discussion progresses, participants from each group write key milestones on designated large posters hanging on the walls. Next, each group discusses emergent patterns from the exchange of ideas—followed by the entire group sharing key findings.

The marked posters hang on the walls for the remainder of the conference, serving as a constant reminder of: *This is where we have all been.*

After the discussions of the past come to a standstill, the conversations move to the present. Before the first day concludes, the group completes a visual diagram or depiction of the current realities, including external trends shaping everyone's personal and professional lives.

Using something visual—for example, words, ideas, tasks—to conceptualize the current times is a difficult activity. "The point of the exercise is *not* to set priorities. Rather it's a step toward dialogue and manageability" (Weisbord and Janoff, 1995: 18).

This concludes the first day of Future Search. Anything more might create overload. Now it is time for participants to go home and allow the day's learning to "soak in."

Day 2—Morning: Focus on Present Trends Continues and Owning Our Actions

At the beginning of the second day, groups are shifted to represent "stakeholder groups." For instance, the composition of the first day groups was heterogeneous, including teachers, administrators, secretaries, and others. The second day encompasses homogenous groups, in other words, teachers would be together, secretarial staff would be together, etcetera.

In the first activity, each group becomes familiar with the specific trends of importance to them. Following further discussion, each group reports on the current trends and what they want to do in the future to respond to those trends.

Next, each group makes a list of "prouds" and "sorries" in relation to the task. Weisbord and Janoff note: The purpose is ownership, not finger pointing.

Day 2—Afternoon: Ideal Future Scenarios and Identify Common Ground

The afternoon presents time for everyone to begin focusing on the future. Returning to diverse groupings, they consider the following question: In ten to twenty years, what will be happening?

Everyone is urged to present an explicit scenario with specifics to overcome any barriers along the way. This activity taps into everyone's unconscious ambitions and goals—bringing to life what they really want.

As each scenario is presented, everyone observes common future themes, potential projects, and unresolved differences. These observations are documents on additional posters, combining comments with similar ideas.

Day 3 —Morning: Ideal Future Scenarios and Identify Common Ground

On the morning of the last day, the whole group reviews the ideas splattered all over the posters. Everyone clarifies and agrees upon each of the values or features that materialized during the previous days.

The items rousing disagreement are reported as "unresolved differences." Once discussion of each item is exhausted, various groups come together to develop short- and long-term plans to disseminate their *fresh* aspirations and goals.

Future search is an excellent meeting design to engage the whole system and co-create purpose. It is only one method for the foundational leader to engage the whole system in experiencing the creation of a shared purpose.

THE WORLD CAFÉ

At the heart of co-creating purpose is deep dialogue with significant effect. In the grand scheme of things, a shared purpose stems from lasting conversation about individual purpose and ways in which purpose becomes a piece of the bigger picture.

One strategy to move individuals toward collective awareness is to engage them in the World Café, a process designed to call people into meaningful conversation. The World Café is a conversational process that promotes a collaborative environment by having participants connect with themselves, with each other, and with a higher purpose.

The World Café evokes the collective intelligence of any group, thus increasing people's capacity for effective action in pursuit of a common purpose. Much of this stems from seven integrated design principles offered by Juanita Brown (2005):

1. *Set the Context:* Clarify the purpose and broad parameters within which the dialogue will unfold.
2. *Create Hospitable Space:* Ensure a welcoming environment and psychological safety that nurtures personal comfort and mutual respect.
3. *Explore Questions That Matter:* Focus collective attention on powerful questions that attract collaborative engagement.
4. *Encourage Everyone's Contributions:* Enliven the relationship between "me" and the "we" by inviting full participation and mutual giving.
5. *Cross-Pollinate and Connect Diverse Perspectives:* Use the living-system dynamics of emergence through intentionally increasing the diversity and density of connections among perspectives while retaining a common focus on core questions.
6. *Listen Together for Patterns, Insights, and Deeper Questions:* Focus shared attention in ways that nurture coherence of thought without losing individual contributions.
7. *Harvest and Share Collective Discoveries:* Make collective knowledge and insight visible and actionable. (40)

To conduct a World Café session, the facilitator breaks the group into smaller groups ranging from four to five people to address the topic. Within each group, one member volunteers to take notes and be the host.

After a specified period, everyone, except the hosts, rotates to the next group at another table. The host provides a brief review of what was discussed with the previous group and the discussion continues with the new group. This continues for several rotations. At the conclusion of the session, each small group shares with the large group.

The World Café is simple, yet powerful. It helps the foundational leader harness the personal stories so many are waiting patiently to share.

8

FOUNDATION #4: FOSTERING EFFECTIVE TEAMS

Future leaders will master teamwork, working with and through others because no one person can master all the sources of information to make good decisions.

—David Ulrich

As declared in the first chapter, "The pendulum will by no means stand still." And with the ever-changing economy, accompanied by so many external pressures, the success of schools stands on the shoulders of effective teams.

This chapter, "Fostering Effective Teams," communicates the last of the four key foundations. The aim of this chapter is not to propose any new theory of teambuilding and group dynamics, much of which has already been covered in past literature, but to draw on specific steps the foundational leader exercises to institutionalize synergetic teamwork throughout the school.

Three phases of team development are outlined later in this chapter. These phases make up the model called "The Proverbial

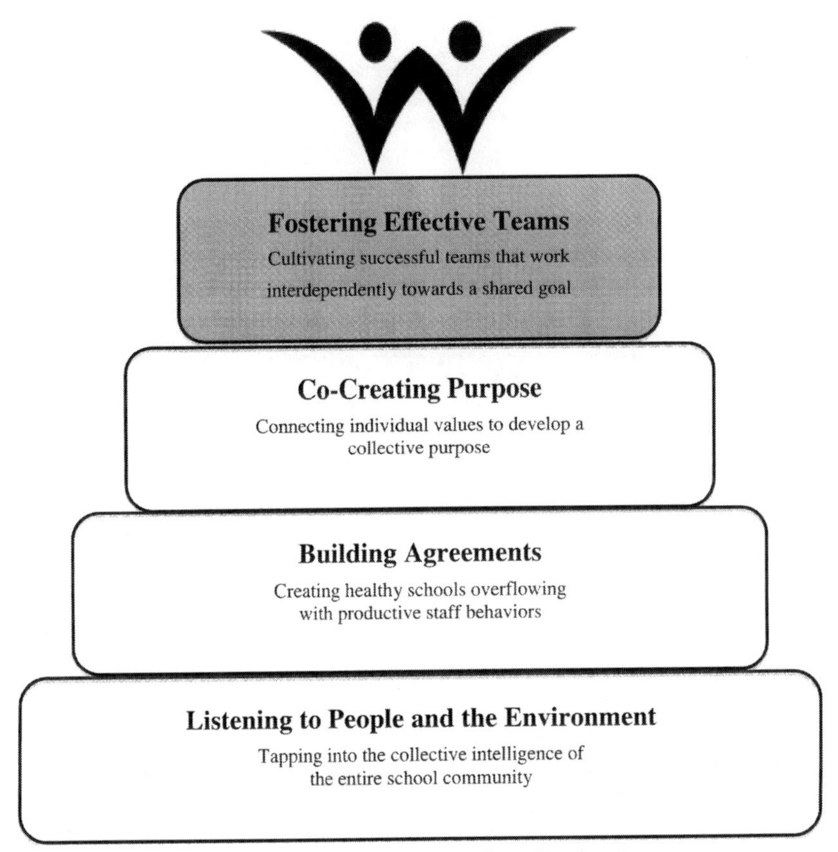

Figure 8.1. Key Foundations Depiction—Fostering Effective Teams

Process." This "proverbial" model is based on three popular sayings:

- "We must become the change we want to see." (Mahatma Gandhi)
- "Tell them, and they will forget. Show them, and they will remember. Involve them and they will learn." (ancient proverb)
- "The way to eat an elephant is one bite at a time." (ancient proverb)

In short, The Proverbial Process presents school leaders with an explicit procedure for teaching and developing staff members' ability to lead teams effectively.

INTERCONNECTIONS BETWEEN THE FOUR KEY FOUNDATIONS

Before plunging into teambuilding, it is necessary to review the ways in which each of the four foundations has built on one another thus far. At the opening of each foundational chapter was a triangular depiction displaying each of the four key foundations in a hierarchical fashion.

Fostering effective teams is at the peak of the triangle because the foundational leader's greatest pride in creating successful, resilient schools is ultimately to produce a school where every team is working effectively and interdependently toward a common purpose. That is his or her deepest ambition.

Thus, it makes sense that the prerequisite to "teams working toward a common purpose" is the development of a shared purpose through the route of co-creating purpose. Tapping into everyone's personal views to construct a purpose that is shared school wide requires an open environment where productive, agreed-on norms support sharing. A genuine shared purpose is not possible if the members of the school do not feel comfortable exchanging ideas or disclosing personal stories.

When agreements are present, they create a culture where disclosure is *the way we do things around here.* Building agreements also serves to guide behavior of the members within each team. In fact, each team may even build self-contained agreements aligned with the school's universal expectations.

And, of course, none of this would be possible without the foundational leader who "listens" to both people and the environment.

WHY FOCUS ON FOSTERING EFFECTIVE TEAMS?

The foundational leader knows skillful teamwork is the key to building successful, resilient schools. Much of a school's success depends on the leader's ability to "work through others because no one person can master all the sources of information to make good decisions" (Ulrich, 1996: 213).

In my research study, *Professional Learning Communities and the Effectiveness of the Teams within Those Communities*, I examined how teams contributed to the institutionalization of collaborative school cultures. Although many published works have argued that team effectiveness was critical to the success of a school, they offered no empirical data to support this view.

In the study, data were gathered from 51 principals and 1,467 teachers in their respective schools. Not surprisingly, the evidence clearly demonstrated the schools exhibiting high levels of collaboration had better functioning teams than their counterparts. This sounded like plain common sense, but the point needed emphasis.

With that in mind, along with a true desire for collaboration as a norm, the foundational leader functions with a frame of mind that dysfunctional teams cannot be tolerated! Leaving teams in a dysfunctional state not only uproots the aim of building a culture of collaboration, but also eventually wreaks havoc in the school.

Why then do so many schools fall short in bringing about change through essential teambuilding?

There are two obvious answers to this question. For one, many have not taken the time to concentrate on each of the foundations outlined in earlier chapters (listening to people and the environment, building agreements, and co-creating purpose). For teams to prosper, each of these underlying principles must manifest.

Secondly, far too many people pay no more than lip service to the concept of effective teams when, in fact, most team members are not schooled in teambuilding techniques. Consequently, the word *team* may be beginning to lose its true meaning.

Far too often, traditional school leaders tend to assemble school members into teams, allocate time lines, and expect high performance and high results. Intentions may be great; however, as many know, building effective teams is no small feat. It is challenging and involved.

The solution is straightforward and takes into account two discrete actions:

1. School leaders must engage the entire school community in building each of the aforementioned key foundations. Without this fundamental groundwork, teams will not have the capacity to operate at their fullest potential.
2. School leaders must allocate time for training both themselves and their staff (especially the team leaders) in the rudiments of team synergy through the "proverbial" model. Effective teambuilding includes providing each team with practical strategies along with the theory to support those strategies.

Without a thorough understanding of effective team characteristics and development processes, many teams continue to operate in a less productive, conventional manner. The foundational leader becomes the vehicle in building staff capacity to lead and operate within highly effective teams.

FOSTERING EFFECTIVE TEAMS: A PROVERBIAL PROCESS

The "Fostering Effective Teams: A Proverbial Process" model (fig. 8.2) is a simple teambuilding construct serving as a springboard for the foundational leader in the pursuit of growing effective teams throughout the school. The steps laid out in this model are practical, functional, and serve as a reminder to the school leader in pursuit of high-functioning teams.

The foundational leader is conscious of the fact that effective teams do not naturally transpire. In actuality, most schools do have structures in place for successful teambuilding, such as time, place, and resources. The missing ingredients are the processes allowing teams to balance their tasks and relationships productively.

Step 1: "We Must Become the Change We Want to See" (Mahatma Gandhi)

Mahatma Gandhi's expression "We must become the change we want to see" is the first step in fostering effective teams. It is the

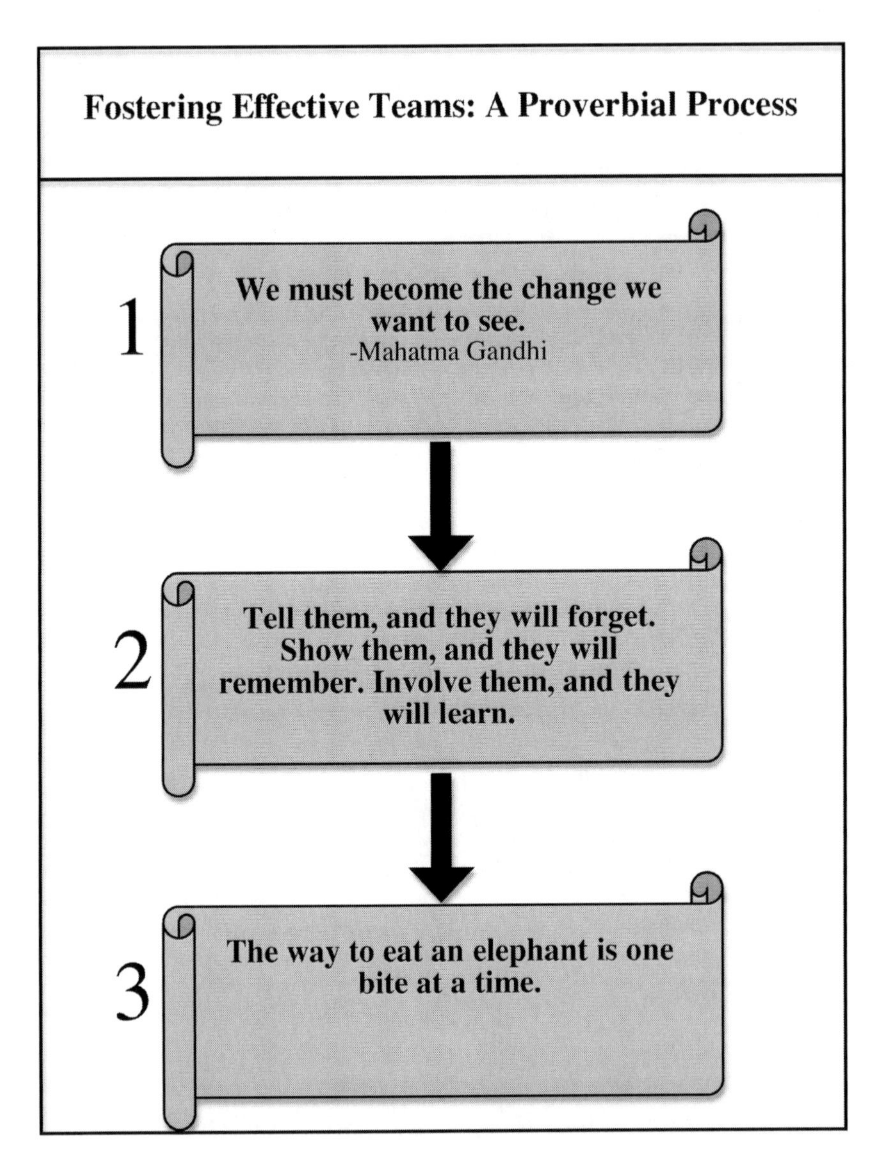

Figure 8.2. Fostering Effective Teams: A Proverbial Process

foundational leader's responsibility to model successful teams by developing his or her highly effective, collaborative teams within the school.

To facilitate team development, the foundational leader first acquires a theoretical understanding of group dynamics and the processes necessary for building effective teams. With that understanding in place, the leader fashions the tools needed to translate the information into concrete action.

For these reasons, the "Do as I say, not as I do" style of leadership falls short. Teambuilding must rest on partnership if a school is to remain or become successful and resilient. A school culture with teamwork and group effort as common practice develops only if the leader provides a model through which the members learn to imagine their ideal team.

The foundational leader frequently asks: Are my own leadership and administrative teams functioning at a level close to the ideal? Do they exemplify the distinctiveness of an effective team?

The answers to these questions are overwhelmingly important because, if the expectation is for teams throughout the school to be functioning at high levels, the leader *must become the change he or she wants to see.*

Step 2: "Involve Them, and They Will Learn"

The next step follows the Chinese proverb: "Tell them, and they will forget. Show them, and they will remember. Involve them, and they will learn."

Because knowledge of teambuilding strategies (and group dynamics) may not be widespread, the foundational leader allocates special time to develop and empower capable team leaders, who must be properly trained to facilitate teamwork. They become the builders of this culture of collaboration.

The following series of activities, if carried out consistently, enables the foundational leader to cultivate effective teamwork throughout the school.

First, the Foundation Leader sets aside training time to model and speak openly about the teambuilding structures, specific processes, and activities expected in the school. Second, the team leaders faithfully articulate these structures and processes to the respective team members and implement them.

As they do so, the foundational leader leads by "walking around" for consistent monitoring of each team's progress, while also observing the environment. Finally, the foundational leader and the team leaders regroup to examine findings, present feedback, and discuss the usefulness of the processes.

Teaching teambuilding is definitely not a one-time workshop. This exercise of teaching teambuilding, having team leaders practice with their respective teams, and coming together for reflection must happen repeatedly. The process has no end because the task of continuously taking teams to a higher plane entails multifaceted study, practice, and reflection.

These activities not only provide an appropriate framework for joint effort, but also help train the team leaders in essential processes for successful teams.

Step 3: "The Way to Eat an Elephant Is One Bite at a Time"

The last of the three steps illustrates the proverb, "The way to eat an elephant is one bite at a time." Viewing the elephant, the larger problem, as the entire scope of fostering effective teams may be setting oneself up for disappointment. Instead, the foundational leader gives the team leaders *one bite at a time*, spoon-feeding them theory and application, allowing time to digest the information through practice, and reflecting on its effectiveness.

Fostering Effective Teams Is a Journey, Not a Destination

To avoid overwhelming people with too many processes, it is profitable to remain focused on a few actions at a time. It would be inappropriate to teach everything at once (Teambuilding 101: The One-Shot Meeting) and expect to see it come to life throughout the school. It requires more effort, accomplished through small, incremental steps.

In his book *One Small Step Can Change Your Life*, Robert Maurer (2004) suggested a Japanese strategy for transformation called *kaizen*. The brain, he contended, was hardwired to resist change; therefore, small steps were needed to build new habits. He quoted the legendary college basketball coach, John Wooden, who said, "When you improve a little each day, eventually big things occur. When you improve conditioning a little each day, eventually you have a big improvement in conditioning. Not tomorrow, not the next day, but eventually a big gain is made. Don't look for the big, quick improvement. Seek the small improvement one day at a time. That's the only way it happens—and when it happens, it lasts" (11).

No quick-fix solution exists. Fostering effective teams takes diligent, purposeful work by the foundational leader because group dynamics are complex and demand consistency. A foundational leader knows building knowledgeable, expert team leaders translates into effective teams.

WHAT ABOUT THE THEORY?

The "proverbial" model is universal and applicable to any teambuilding theory or process. Each of the steps is suitable for any teambuilding skill sets the leader chooses.

Although the model is all-purpose, the foundational leader often applies one particular teambuilding theory throughout the process of fostering effective teams. Specifically, the preferred theory is Thomas Harvey and Bonita Drolet's (2004) seventeen characteristics of effective teams.

The 17 characteristics provide the foundational leader with a vehicle for the construction of more productive and long-lasting teams throughout the school. They also provide the team members with a conceptual picture to guide their practical application.

The foundational leader focuses on teambuilding by coupling the seventeen characteristics of effective teams with the "proverbial" model. When united, these models create success not only for the teams within the school, but also for the school as a whole.

Seventeen Characteristics of Effective Teams

Harvey and Drolet posited that the nurturing of each characteristic sparked high degrees of teamness. They placed the characteristics into four categories, as follows:

Category #1: Purpose of the Team

1. Common Identity and Tenets
2. Common Tasks
3. Sense of Potency/Success

Category #2: Composition of the Team

4. Clear Definition of Team Membership
5. Recognition of Individual Contributions
6. Balanced Roles

Category #3: Interaction Between Members of the Team

7. Mutual Trust
8. Sense of Relationship
9. Open/Direct Conflict
10. Common Base of Information
11. High-Level Question-Asking and Listening
12. Healthy Level of Stress
13. Toleration of Errors
14. Flexibility and Responsiveness

Category #4: Structure and Context of the Team

15. Clear Understanding/Acceptance of Group Structure
16. Periodic Attention to Group Maintenance
17. Recognition and Mitigation of Outside Forces

Purpose of the Team

Purpose of the team composed the first area of the seventeen characteristics of effective teams. Shared purpose is necessary for teams to make systemic changes toward collaboration and a common commitment.

Often, teams are unsuccessful because many fall prey to the paradox of group identity because their members do not feel connected to the team. When members do not share a connection with the team and its purpose, those members may not fully support the direction of the team, causing frustration and dissatisfaction. On the other hand, when members feel connected, they take more ownership in decisions, processes, and changes.

Teams operating without a sense of purpose often suffer from a variety of dysfunctions, such as burnout, dissatisfaction, low morale, and low productivity. However, institutions operating with a sense of purpose create environments where individuals are empowered, forward-looking, and intrinsically motivated. They accomplish tasks both more quickly and more efficiently.

Composition of the Team

The second area, composition of the team, affirms that if the team is uncertain about team membership and composition, individuals struggle to give up part of themselves in order to become a meaningful part of the team. Harvey and Drolet (2004) noted: "If a group is to function as a team, its members must share a clear and explicit knowledge of the persons who are and are not part of the group. When the boundaries are unclear—when individuals are sometimes in, sometimes out–the group is less a team and more an arena for discussion" (18–19).

Figuratively speaking, a clear definition of team membership serves as a container for the group.

A team's performance depends on the qualities of the individuals who are performing the task. An ideal team composition contains competent and knowledgeable members, diversity that represents the relevant parts of the school, and the necessary group process skills to operate effectively (Levi, 2001).

Interaction Between Members of the Team

Interaction is the third area of Harvey and Drolet's seventeen characteristics of effective teams. How team members interact plays a vital role in the success and effectiveness of the team. Overall, the category of interaction is concerned with positive interpersonal relationships between and among members. These relationships nurture an open, inclusive environment. Creating an environment within groups and teams involves vulnerability and risk taking.

A prerequisite to healthy communication within a group includes the building of trust, getting to know one another, and permitting disagreement. Similar to the process of building agreements school wide, teams must also be prepared to overcome the inevitability of conflict within the team. Immediately moving to the task without following through with actions to build positive collegial relations will not provide an open, inclusive communication environment.

Structure and Context of the Team

The final category comprises the team's structure and context. Commitment is a significant element for team development and, if the structure of the team is perceived as unproductive or non-inclusive, members struggle to buy in and support the team's direction.

It is important for teams to check their structure and process frequently by stepping back and reorganizing. For example, many teams struggle with balancing the tasks and group functions. In lieu of moving forward on the task and overlooking personal feelings, time must be set aside to attend to relationships among team members.

SURVEY OF TEAM CHARACTERISTICS

Harvey and Drolet also offered a survey instrument, Survey of Team Characteristics (fig. 8.3), designed to develop teambuilding capacity by providing leaders with a practical tool to measure the existence of the characteristics defining effective teams. Each question contained in the survey represents a respective characteristic. For instance, question #1 represents the first characteristic, *common identity and tenets.*

In 1996, R. Corkrum, a doctoral student, employed a descriptive and correlational research design to validate the content and reliability of the Survey of Team Characteristics. His research revealed a positive relationship among all seventeen characteristics and each of the three variables: effective teamwork, positive team interactions, and teamness.

If a particular school was focusing on building effective teams, it could determine evidence of each of Harvey and Drolet's seventeen characteristics of effective teams by means of the survey. For example a school might render information similar to the data displayed in figure 8.4.

As illustrated, teachers are listed in the left-hand column and their ratings of each of the seventeen characteristics run across the row. The far right-hand column represents the overall mean for each respective teacher. The bottom of each column reveals the overall mean for each of the seventeen characteristics.

According to the data in the figure, this particular school demonstrated high means for the following three characteristics:

- *Question #4:* Everyone understands who belongs as part of the group and who does not. (Mean of 7.74)

Survey of Team Characteristics

Directions:

Listed below are 17 suggested team characteristics. Within any work group these characteristics may occur in varying degrees. Using the scale illustrated below to answer questions 1 through 17, mark the rating, 1 through 9, which most closely reflects the extent that each characteristic describes the groups and/or teams you belong to.

Not at all characteristic of the group	**Somewhat characteristic of the group**	**Very characteristic of the group**
1 ____ 2 ____ 3 ____	4 ____ 5 ____ 6 ____	7 ____ 8 ____ 9

	1	*2*	*3*	*4*	*5*	*6*	*7*	*8*	*9*
1. Group members share a common identity and work from a common set of beliefs.									
2. Group members work together (as opposed to working in isolation) in order to accomplish tasks.									
3. Group members believe the group is capable and will be successful.									
4. Everyone understands who belongs as part of the group and who does not (i.e. team membership).									
5. The roles or contributions of individual group members are openly recognized and appreciated.									
6. Tasks are balanced throughout the group with each member getting some "piece of the action."									
7. Feelings of trust exist within the group and among group members.									
8. The group's work environment is joyful or positive.									
9. Conflict among group members is openly dealt with; it is not allowed to fester.									
10. All group members have access and openly share information; no one is left "out of the loop."									
11. During work sessions, group discourse is marked by high levels of listening as well as question-asking.									
12. Stress is managed by the group so that it is not so high as to cause group paralysis and not so low that it doesn't induce productive group work.									
13. Risk-taking is encouraged while errors are tolerated and seen as opportunities for growth.									
14. Group members share a willingness to be flexible and a desire to be responsive to external input.									
15. Group members understand and accept the group's organizational structure and operational format.									
16. The group engages in periodic "time out" or "maintenance sessions" to address individual concerns about process or behaviors.									
17. The group is aware of external factors and is pragmatic in its approach.									

Figure 8.3. Survey of Team Characteristics

Teacher	Characteristics of Teams Survey Question																	
	1	2	3	4	5	6	7	8	9	10	11	12	13	14	15	16	17	Mean
1	7	5	6	4	4	5	4	5	7	7	6	7	8	7	6	3	5	5.64706
2	7	6	7	7	7	6	6	6	5	8	8	8	8	7	8	7	8	7
3	8	7	7	7	7	7	6	6	5	5	7	7	6	6	7	5	6	6.41176
4	7	7	8	7	7	6	6	7	7	7	6	6	7	7	6	5	6	6.58824
5	9	9	9	9	9	9	9	9	9	9	9	9	9	9	9	9	9	9
6	9	9	9	8	9	9	9	8	9	8	9	6	9	9	8	9	8	8.52941
7	7	7	7	9	9	8	8	7	7	8	7	7	7	8	8	6	7	7.47059
8	7	7	8	9	5	7	9	5	5	6	7	8	7	8	7	8	7	7.05882
9	9	8	9	9	9	9	9	9	9	9	9	9	9	9	9	9	9	8.94118
10	6	9	7	8	9	7	9	7	8	9	8	9	9	8	8	5	8	7.88235
11	8	8	9	9	9	9	9	9	9	9	9	9	9	8	9	9	9	8.82353
12	9	9	9	9	9	9	9	9	9	9	9	9	9	9	9	9	9	9
13	9	9	9	9	9	7	9	7	7	9	9	8	9	7	9	7	9	8.35294
14	8	8	8	8	8	8	8	8	8	8	8	8	8	8	8	8	8	8
15	5	6	7	9	8	7	8	8	5	7	8	7	7	8	8	9	8	7.35294
16	5	6	6	6	8	6	6	8	6	8	6	8	7	8	6	9	8	6.88235
17	6	4	6	2	3	5	2	3	3	6	6	6	5	7	6	4	8	4.82353
18	5	5	5	8	5	2	4	6	5	7	6	5	5	6	5	4	7	5.29412
19	8	5	9	9	6	7	9	9	8	8	8	7	7	8	8	1	6	7.23529
20	6	7	7	9	7	3	5	7	4	5	7	6	5	6	5	3	5	5.70588
21	9	9	9	9	9	7	9	9	9	9	9	9	9	9	9	9	9	8.88235
22	9	9	9	9	9	9	9	5	8	9	8	7	8	8	9	7	7	8.17647
23	9	9	8	9	9	9	9	9	9	7	7	7	8	9	8	7	7	8.23529
24	7	7	8	8	8	7	8	9	7	8	9	9	9	9	9	6	9	8.05882
25	7	8	8	8	8	9	8	8	8	8	8	8	9	9	8	8	7	8.05882
26	6	3	6	9	2	1	3	1	1	4	4	2	2	5	7	1	8	3.82353
27	7	7	8	8	8	7	8	8	9	6	9	6	4	8	5	9	8	7.35294
28	7	6	8	8	7	7	6	7	7	6	7	7	6	7	7	7	7	6.88235
29	7	2	3	7	2	1	9	4	2	5	9	2	5	7	na	4	4	4.5625
30	7	8	9	6	7	7	9	8	9	8	8	7	6	6	6	7	6	7.29412
31	8	5	9	9	7	8	9	8	8	9	9	8	8	8	8	8	8	8.05882
32	4	5	6	2	4	7	7	8	6	7	6	5	5	6	5	6	5	5.52941
33	8	6	6	8	8	6	7	6	3	6	7	3	3	5	3	3	3	5.35294
34	6	3	5	8	7	2	5	5	5	8	6	6	6	6	4	7	5	5.52941
35	8	9	9	8	8	7	8	7	7	7	7	8	8	8	8	7	8	7.76471
	7.257	6.771	7.514	7.743	7.143	6.571	7.371	7	6.657	7.4	7.571	6.943	7.029	7.514	7.206	6.429	7.171	7.13036

Figure 8.4. Characteristics of Teams Survey Data

- *Question #11:* During work sessions, group discourse is marked by high levels of listening as well as question-asking. (Mean of 7.57)
- *Question #3:* Group members believe the group is capable and will be successful. (Mean of 7.51)

On the contrary, the school scored lowest in the following characteristics:

- *Question #16:* The group engages in periodic "time out" or "maintenance sessions" to address individual concerns about process or behaviors. (Mean of 6.43)
- *Question #6:* Tasks are balanced throughout the group and among group members. (Mean of 6.57)
- *Question #9:* Conflict among group members is openly dealt with; it is not allowed to fester. (Mean of 6.66)

As the foundational leader works with team leaders, involving them, so they will learn, they celebrate their high scoring characteristics. The foundational leader celebrates whenever possible. It is also an opportunity to intervene in the low scoring areas.

In the case above, the three lowest scoring questions (#16, #6, and #9) speak as an abstraction. The scores revealed the people and the environment were saying something and asking for help. In reviewing the data, the foundational leader—alongside team leaders—might come to two conclusions.

First, a low score on question #6, Balanced Roles, may indicate teams are assigning a majority of the tasks to only a select few. This could upset those taking on a majority of the workload, while others sit back and watch—so to speak. A problem is created when these "workhorses" are unfortunately allowing these feelings to fester (question #9).

Second, if the roles aren't balanced and anger and frustration festers, problems arise. This, coupled with failure to take periodic "time outs" to address individual concerns about process or behaviors (question #16), results in damaged relationships. The teams continue to spiral downward.

In this situation, the foundational leader might train team leaders—through the "Proverbial Process," of course—in activities to ensure roles are balanced within and across teams. It would also be an opportune time for the leader to present further actions to aid the ongoing process of building agreements. These agreements need to be revisited frequently as a type of "time out."

THE FIVE MOST ESSENTIAL CHARACTERISTICS OF EFFECTIVE TEAMS

Trying to deal with the seventeen characteristics may be daunting to any school leader with a tight schedule, particularly since team dynamics are complex. During Corkrum's (1996) research, he found a more effective way to measure the current state of a team through the "Five Fast ID Elements" to examine when fostering effective teams. Those elements were:

1. Clear Understanding/Acceptance of Group Structure
2. Common Tasks
3. Open/Direct Conflict
4. Mutual Trust
5. Toleration of Error

The foundational leader is well advised to "digest" this second list slowly—*the way to eat an elephant is one bite at a time.*

The five fast ID elements will be discussed further in the next chapter, and play a major part in the four key foundations assessment introduced in chapter 10, "Becoming a Progressive Practitioner."

9

METHODS FOR FORMING EFFECTIVE TEAMS: DEVELOPING THE FIVE FAST ID ELEMENTS

It's easy to get good players. Getting them to play together, that's the hard part.

—Casey Stengel

The "proverbial" model is geared toward helping team leaders facilitate highly effective teams. Its argument is straightforward: If team leaders within a school are better skilled in teambuilding and group dynamics, their respective teams are more likely to function at higher levels.

Everyone has differing levels of understanding in respect to teambuilding. Some are experts, while it may be uncharted territory for others. The aim in fostering effective teams is to create a common set of procedures and processes—bringing together every proficient level in the art of teambuilding. Foundational leaders must have time to train and develop team leaders by explicitly discussing and demonstrating expected teambuilding structures and processes.

For the school in its infancy stages of teambuilding, the five fast ID elements are a great place to start. Again, those elements are:

1. Clear Understanding/Acceptance of Group Structure
2. Common Tasks
3. Open/Direct Conflict
4. Mutual Trust
5. Toleration of Error

These five fundamental characteristics make perfect sense. Think about it: Exemplar teams understand and accept their structure, they work on common tasks, get along with one another, and are not afraid to try groundbreaking ideas.

Of course, this is all easier said than done. Remember the added complexities of diversity in cultures, worldviews, attitudes, values, and experiences. Leadership, no matter the venue, is difficult. The same is true for those members of the school who are charged with leading teams.

Because it isn't a good idea to bite off more than one can chew, the foundational leader begins fostering effective teams by focusing on one or more of the five fast ID elements. Each of the elements will be briefly introduced in this chapter, followed by discrete strategies that can help bring them into fruition.

FIVE FAST ID ELEMENT #1

Clear understanding/acceptance of group structure is the first of the five fast ID elements. "Group structure" refers to the way tasks are divided within a team and the processes the team uses in planning and decision-making. "The key factor in any structure," Thomas Harvey and Bonita Drolet (2004) wrote, "is buy-in of the members. Vertical or horizontal, leaderless, collaborative, or authoritarian—any structure can work if team members value the structure and understand and accept their role in it" (30).

Strategy #1: Teach Proper Facilitation

Team leaders need to be explicitly taught correct ways to facilitate meetings. Facilitation ability, or lack thereof, ultimately influences the effectiveness of the team. When team leaders are better skilled in facilitation, their teams are superior in creating the synergy necessary for success in both tasks and relationships. Schooling in facilitation is really one of the most urgent responsibilities for the foundational leader in the "proverbial" model.

For continuous growth, team members must participate in different activities to build healthy relationships, establish clear and concise goals, and solve problems. Unfortunately, many team leaders lack formal training on the "ins and outs" of facilitation, which leads to team dysfunction, such as tasks being completed insufficiently, rambling participants, and personality conflicts. The list goes on and on.

Similar to the foundational leader's ability to listen through a variety of large- and small-group processes, team leaders need their own techniques to help guide the group to accomplish its goals. A few resources that the foundational leader references when teaching team leader facilitation are:

- *The 1978 Annual Handbook for Group Facilitators* by J. William Pfeiffer and John Jones (1978). There are dozens of meeting designs in this extensive resource to help facilitators generate more useful agendas for teams.
- *The Skilled Facilitator* by Roger Schwartz (2002). Included in his work are theories and practical strategies to increase group effectiveness.
- *The Ultimate Training Workshop Handbook* by Bruce Klatt (1999). This comprehensive guide serves as a toolkit for anyone who leads meeting, workshops, or training programs.
- *The Secrets of Facilitation* by Michael Wilkinson (2004). This book provides facilitators with "secrets" to guiding people in creating, understanding, and accepting solutions.

Strategy #2: Develop Team Names, Pictures, and Spirit

Metaphorically, people need to develop a "container" feeling within their teams. This container helps members share a common identity and a sense of belonging. Without that feeling, members will not be connected to the team and its decisions.

One way to generate team membership and spirit is to have each team choose a name. This could be a favorite college, a mascot, or other theme. Requiring the teams to designate a name presents an opportunity for the team leader to try out new techniques to generate and winnow the team's ideas.

Another way to give people a sense of belonging is through team pictures. After all, a picture is worth a thousand words. Think about a photograph of friends and family that invokes a feeling of togetherness. The same is true when a team poses for a photograph. Pictures not only spawn great memories, they also represent something bigger, something permanent.

Another strategy the foundational leader practices to appeal to team spirit is team challenges. These could happen throughout the year leading to some incentive for the winners. Maybe "Team Tigers" win the end of the year award. Clearly defined team membership, the feeling of belonging, and spirit are important in teams.

Strategy #3: Meet in a Formal Setting Regularly

Teams should meet on a regular basis. This is the critical time when they tackle key issues, make decisions that improve the team and the school, and build healthy relationships. Once a month might not be sufficient. It is the foundational leader's responsibility to designate explicit time for teams to meet within the school day.

With the advent of technology, many teams in schools may fall prey to becoming virtual teams—e-mailing one another to communicate and make decisions, even if they are located in close proximity to one another. Although "virtual teams" have a place in education and schools, teams are better able to build supporting relationships and participate in inclusive meeting designs during face-to-face meetings.

To help with meetings, team leaders should designate and rotate assigned roles for each member. This can take the form of facilitators, timekeepers, and scribes.

FIVE FAST ID ELEMENT #2

The second of the five fast ID elements is "common tasks." Unified teams complete their tasks together. Team members come together and draw from one another's strengths because "Groups lacking a common task are simply involved in parallel play; they do the same thing, not together, but side-by-side" (Harvey and Drolet, 2004: 16). In addition, cohesive teams are involved in tasks that are complex enough to lean on cooperative efforts rather than individual efforts.

Fostering effective teams happens school wide when teams work interdependently toward a common purpose. The same is true for each team. Each of its members must work interdependently toward common tasks that support the school's shared purpose. Without common tasks, the need for "teams" doesn't exist.

Strategy #1: Assign Task Forces

A majority of teams in schools focus on tasks, such as developing common assessments, planning lessons, and analyzing data. These are all important, but the foundational leader takes "common tasks" to the next level.

More often than not, teams in schools don't participate in the planning of major school wide events. In fact, nearly all of the most important school tasks are assigned to the same few individuals. To develop potency in teams and provide "common tasks," the foundational leader assigns each team a collection of major activities they will be required to plan, communicate, and implement. This also gives teams and their members a chance to network with other staff members throughout the school.

Strategy #2: Teach Teams About Data Analysis and Action Research

Schools are data rich and information poor. The foundational leader teaches others how to work together to analyze the hordes of data and decide on interventions to be put in place. This can be accomplished through the action research model, which is thoroughly explained in chapter 10, "Becoming a Progressive Practitioner."

Throughout the school year, teams are bombarded with student achievement data from state test scores, district benchmarks to grade-level assessments, and teacher-generated quizzes. Data overload bogs down teams in their ability to determine student gaps and the specific steps to rise above them. Teams need more direction in collaboratively breaking down data and determining specific, manageable goals, a common task they execute throughout the school year.

Strategy #3: Develop S.M.A.R.T. Goals

Chapter 10 introduces the S.M.A.R.T. goal worksheet. This worksheet keeps teams focused and working together on projects—no matter the size. It is an easy way for teams to organize their tasks, delegate responsibilities, and meet deadlines. In fact, if the teams are better able to extrapolate interventions in response to data, they can plan their actions using the S.M.A.R.T. goals worksheet.

When a project or task is sketched out on paper, its completion is more tangible. It is no different than one's pursuit of accomplishing a personal goal. When the desired outcome is written down, it becomes easier to achieve. The S.M.A.R.T. goal worksheet allows team members to determine not only an overarching goal but also specific steps to accomplish this target.

FIVE FAST ID ELEMENT #3

Open/direct conflict is the third of the five fast ID elements. Conflict in teams can be both positive and negative. Prevailing over conflict productively plays a significant role in building effective teams because it builds trust and stronger collegial relationships. According to Schwartz (2002), "An effective group considers conflict a natural part of group life; if it is managed well, conflict improves members' ability to accomplish their task, work together, and contribute to personal growth" (24).

Conflict in teams arises when differences among members become apparent. A negative outcome is not predestined by any means, and diversity may contribute to the development of either productive or dysfunctional dynamics. The foundational leader teaches others to re-channel conflict with a view to promoting improvement. How members deal with conflict is a good measure of how effective they are as a team.

Strategy #1: Develop Team Norms

Conflict within a team is to be expected. Many times, teams experience internal struggles (e.g., rumors, innuendo, ineffective processes, and neglecting relationship behaviors) without taking the necessary steps to gain perspective on what did and did not work. This failure to learn from their struggles, in turn, impedes progress.

One strategy to help teams overcome such problems includes the collective development of clear team norms. Jointly developed group norms are most effective when the whole group contributes to the process. These norms create a tangible framework the group can revisit at any time. That is, the periodic reexamination of group norms can be considered a "periodic attention to group maintenance."

Traditionally, group norms speak to the manner in which individuals handle conflict and support a means of communication in which input and a diversity of perspectives are valued. These complexities are derived from the assortment of points of view and worldviews members bring to the team. Norms eliminate ambiguity, delineate expected conduct, and encourage a collective commitment.

For practical purposes, Richard DuFour et al. (2006) offered tips for creating team norms:

1. Each team should create its own norms.
2. Norms should be stated more as commitments to act or behave in certain ways than as beliefs.
3. Norms should be reviewed at the beginning and end of each meeting for at least six months.
4. Teams should formally evaluate their effectiveness at least twice a year.
5. Teams should focus on a few essential norms rather than creating an extensive laundry list.
6. Violations of team norms must be addressed. (106)

Interestingly, Frank LaFasto and Carl Larson (2001) conducted extensive research on teams and received the following comments from team members regarding shortcomings in relationships:

1. We need to give feedback and confront each other more directly.
2. People must be more open about the way they feel and more comfortable giving honest criticism to peers, subordinates, and superiors.
3. Create a level of trust to foster mutual feedback. (34–35)

LaFasto and Larson's research revealed that team members must give special attention to giving and receiving feedback in team norms.

Just as building agreements is *foundational* in the pursuit of successful, resilient schools, developing productive norms within teams is just as important. The school as a whole probably has a much different personality than the personalities of its respective teams.

Strategy #2: Frequently Revisit Team Norms

A multitude of reasons exist for why it is beneficial for teams to evaluate and reflect on their processes and structures. First, the data that emerged from my dissertation research conveyed that this practice rarely happened in school teams. Yet, brief "time outs" are significant as a team tries to gain perspective on what did and did not work.

Frequently revisiting team norms is analogous to Harvey and Drolet's (2004) sixteenth characteristic, periodic attention to group maintenance. The foundational leader not only teaches the importance of "time out," but he or she also demonstrates to the team leaders the exercise of "getting off the dance floor and going to the balcony." This will also help teams get a better understanding of the dynamics unfolding within a team.

FIVE FAST ID ELEMENT #4

The fourth of the five fast ID elements is "mutual trust." Trust in teams is imperative. It provides roots for the team without which the team will fall to the ground. Without trust, a team will be unable to operate because of decreased communication, less cooperation, and more conflicts that are harder to resolve (Levi, 2001). On the other hand, if team members trust each other, they will be willing to open up and state their beliefs and feelings about the team's issues.

In a study conducted by James Kouzes and Barry Posner (2002), several groups participated in a variety of role-playing exercises that focused on trust. Following the activities, the members of the high-trust groups responded:

1. Members were more open about feelings.
2. Members experienced greater clarity about the group's basic problems and goals.
3. Members searched for alternative courses of action.
4. Members reported greater levels of mutual influence on outcomes, satisfaction with the meeting, motivation to implement decisions, and closeness as a management team as a result of the meeting.

Although building trust is important, it also requires disclosure from members, and this may be difficult for many. Teams have to come together for multiple structured opportunities and gain trust over time.

Strategy #1: Icebreakers, Games, or Activities

Team icebreakers, games, or activities are a great method for building trust within teams. They can help with the team's function, as well as its maintenance. Some are quick and easy, while others are concentrated and more time consuming. It all depends on the expected outcome of the team. These activities are fun and helpful in team effectiveness but they cannot supplant the routine tasks of a team. In other words, teams can't just play all the time.

If the aim is to build relationships, the icebreaker should engage the team in discovery and disclosure. On the other hand, if the aim is to get creative juices flowing before a major brainstorming session, the activity should challenge the team.

Team activities are easy to facilitate in the "proverbial" model. As the team leaders meet with the foundational leader in preparation for their own approaching team meeting, they participate in the activity. It is modeled for them. Multiple resources can be used for examples of icebreakers, such as:

1. *Group Activities* by Mary Keene and Bradley Erford (2007).
2. *The Big Book of Teambuilding Games* by John Newstrom and Edward Scannell (1998).
3. *Team Games for Trainers* by Carolyn Nilson (1993).
4. *101 Ways to Make Meetings Active* by Mel Silberman (1999).
5. *201 Icebreakers: Group Mixers, Warm-Ups, Energizers, and Playful Activities* by Edie West (1997).

Strategy #2: Celebrate Frequently

The school culture must cherish celebrations of teams and their members. When teams celebrate frequently, their members build trust. These memorable moments can be informal through compliments and "thank you's" or formal through some type of ceremony. Working collaboratively on projects and tasks takes hard work and it should be recognized. The tears and laughter bring out the human side of the work.

Strategy #3: Off-Site Retreats

Meetings that take place at the school can become repetitive. Occasionally, teams must expand their meetings beyond the school through off-site retreats. It is a great way to energize the team, commence a new project, or spark new ideas.

Many people state that when they are brainstorming ideas, they can move to another room in the house and more ideas come. The same is true for groups of people. Sometimes, teams or entire staffs need to change their environment when tackling problems.

Off-site retreats can help teams generate new solutions, create new ways of working together, and build stronger bonds. It also helps to be away so there are no disturbances with day-to-day dealings. Merianne Liteman, Sheila Campbell, and Jeffrey Liteman (2006) wrote a great book on retreats titled *Retreats that Work.* Team leaders planning to institute an off-site retreat should have this resource handy.

FIVE FAST ID ELEMENT #5

"Toleration of errors" is the last of the five fast ID elements. Effective teams sponsor creativity and innovation. However, as Harvey and Drolet (2004) held, "When we seek creative, new opportunities, we must be prepared for mistakes. Organizations claiming to be 'error-free' do not spark the employees to innovation or risk-taking; instead, they are toxic, choking off ventures that involve any risk" (27–28).

Individuals are more likely to apply creativity when they perceive strong support from the leader. Creativity and innovation may never manifest if the environment does not support it. An important element of the toleration of errors is the ability to give and receive constructive feedback, which is a key teamwork skill. Feedback is necessary if individuals are to grow and improve their performance.

How a group or team gives and receives feedback establishes the group climate within which mistakes are accepted. Accepting, learning, and growing from the mistakes that occur in an environment that fosters inventiveness entails the ability to give and receive constructive feedback.

Team members must be able to share personal practices and provide feedback without damaging relationships. By contrast, those members who are not genuinely open about their mistakes and weaknesses make it impossible to build a foundation of trust.

Strategy #1: Empower Teams

The foundational leader understands the team is the keystone of school improvement. With this in mind, teams must be given the chance to mature and constantly try out new things. As teams participate in task forces—making critical decisions for the school—they need to be trusted with their decision-making abilities.

When the foundational leader is uncertain about a particular decision the team suggests, the response should be, "What was the process in coming to this conclusion?" If the team leader worked with the team and others by means of sound processes or techniques, it might be beneficial to support the decision. Over time, the teams and their members will grasp the notion that they are empowered if they take the time to do it right.

It is critical that the foundational leader empowers teams through task forces and other responsibilities, but also clearly delineates upfront any boundaries or limitations (e.g., monetary and time resources).

The foundational leader empowers teams by giving them freedom to feel ownership in the accomplishment of their own tasks, as well as tasks that benefit the entire school. It is also explicitly shared that it is natural to make mistakes. It is an inherent feature of new ideas and change.

Strategy #2: Tell Stories

Storytelling can drive change in teams. The foundational leader constantly paints a picture for others, sharing how teams and individuals are given authority, and how they thrive in the face of challenge. Of course, the path isn't perfect because they have to use trial and error to get to the result.

Stories like these link people together. They share a narrative that creates new traditions, inspires others, and develops a shared identity. When teams hear stories of empowerment and are given important tasks, they are more likely to come together and make a difference in the school.

Included in this chapter were multiple specific strategies to help the foundational leader in fostering effective teams through the five fast ID elements. Those schools that may already be in more advanced stages of teambuilding will want to try further activities and explore the other twelve characteristics offered by Harvey and Drolet.

The only way to become better at teambuilding is to try new things. Some will work and others won't. That is perfectly OK.

II

FROM THEORY TO PRACTICE

To recognize opportunity is the difference between success and failure.

—Unknown

INTRODUCTORY REMARKS

Thus far, we have discussed the four key foundations necessary for building successful, resilient schools. The utmost feat in carrying out the foundations is when teams throughout the school are working effectively and interdependently toward a shared purpose. A variety of theories accompanied by processes were presented to help move schools toward that ideal.

Now, the objective is to create a self-designing system where the leader has the capacity to use various methods and can move each of the four key foundations from paper to practice.

Chapter 10 discusses just how to do that. It is what the foundational leader calls becoming a progressive practitioner. Included in this chapter is the Four Key Foundations Assessment—a tool designed to determine the level of maturity for each of the foundations. Its goal is to turn the foundational leader into a "theoretical practitioner," a kind of fountainhead of mental models informed by cutting-edge theories, data analysis, and purposeful action.

As a progressive practitioner, the foundational leader constantly reframes situations by attending fearlessly to each of the foundations, facilitating interventions, collecting data, delving into theory . . . and *reframing*. The notion that "this is the way we have always done it around here and this is how it's going to be" is a hollow pretense.

The final chapter, titled "Final Thoughts," is a call to action. Tomorrow, two weeks from now, or next year will not cut it. The best time is *now*. The foundational leader needs to adopt a proactive stance immediately if he or she is to close the "knowing-doing" gap. Successful, resilient schools are led by foundational leaders who think and act accordingly.

10

BECOMING A PROGRESSIVE PRACTITIONER: APPLYING THE FOUR KEY FOUNDATIONS

Somewhere, something incredible is waiting to be known.

—Carl Sagan

Becoming a progressive practitioner governs how the foundational leader moves the four key foundations from theory to practice through the application of action research. In action research, the foundational leader uses a reflective approach to progressive problem-solving in the midst of change or adaptation to change.

Schools must not be allowed to develop naturally. The foundational leader recognizes this and intervenes when necessary in order to take charge of the school's development (especially around each of the foundations). The foundational leader is a progressive practitioner, engaging in critical thinking and employing systematic data-driven methods for problem-solving. When this occurs, the two titles—foundational leader and progressive practitioner—become interchangeable.

CHAPTER 10

THE FOUNDATIONAL LEADER AS A PROGRESSIVE PRACTITIONER

The main objective of the foundational leader, somewhat like a "theoretical practitioner," is to connect knowledge with action—in other words, to close the "knowing-doing" gap. Merely knowing the importance of building the four key foundations for success is insufficient. Actions have to match words.

What separates foundational leaders from run-o'-the-mill school leaders is their practiced ability to discern what might or might not work. When they do well, they know exactly why; when they fail, they also know why. In fact, they feel more comfortable failing and knowing why than succeeding and missing the point. They are adept at thinking of long-term development because the four foundations aren't a fly-by-night operation.

The "Knowledge/Success Matrix" model (fig. 10.1) depicts this mental process. It is made up of four quadrants associating "success" and "failure" with "knowing" and "not knowing," relative to the outcome. Quadrant 1 represents a successful change initiative linked to *known* specific steps. The fourth quadrant represents an unsuccessful initiative, linked to no specific steps.

By moving their schools one small step at a time, foundational leaders are able to identify a systematic course of action. They can document actions, analyze the data, and determine if a practice ought to be continued. They are always aware of their actions and the exact outcomes of those actions. The foundational leader spends most of the time operating in the first quadrant—experiencing success and understanding what exactly led to that success.

A recent example is the current accountability system in education, which purports to encourage all schools to make progress and to allow states and districts to penalize those schools consistently failing to meet expectations. For this to work, any school showing progress should provide evidence of success and the school leader ought to know how to react. This is frequently not what happens. All too often, school leaders tend to cross their fingers and wish for the

	Successful	Unsuccessful
Known	Quadrant 1 Known and Successful	Quadrant 2 Known and Unsuccessful
Unknown	Quadrant 3 Unknown and Successful	Quadrant 4 Unknown and Unsuccessful

Figure 10.1. Knowledge/Success Matrix

best—awaiting the release of the test scores—something of a crapshoot. The problem with such an approach is no one can pinpoint the exact interventions leading to the results.

Successful or not, the foundational leader knows what led to the result. Tested theories are carefully gathered, formulated into new hypotheses, and logically applied to ideas. This is the only avenue to quadrants 1 and 2 ("known and successful" and "known and unsuccessful"). Staying in those quadrants enables the foundational leader to replicate the techniques and strategies profiting the school, while discontinuing the ineffective ones. This is how the school continually moves toward the outcomes expected of it.

CHAPTER 10

ACTION RESEARCH MODEL

Typically, the foundational leader affirms that school leadership and development have to be based on science; the school is a research laboratory, and no research into school development is more fitting than *action research.* From the unknown, in short, the foundational leader wants to move the entire school to the known. Therefore, the action research model weaves theory into reflection and practice. This structures the foundational leader's effort to improve strategy.

Anyone can profit from action research. It doesn't require comprehensive knowledge of statistics—correlations, causal comparisons, or ethnographic methodology. Action research can be broken down into six segments:

1. Frame
2. Assessment
3. Feedback
4. Diagnosis
5. Planning
6. Action

Figure 10.2 illustrates these segments in an action research cycle. It's an ongoing process moving toward quadrant 1 of the Knowledge/Success Matrix—the highest quadrant where the reasons for success are known. Moreover, a "learning loop" corresponds to each segment listed above. The foundational leader completes the first loop after facilitating each segment. Action is then taken, followed by periodic "rests" to evaluate the effectiveness of the action.

At that point, the leader asks "What's really going on here?" and views the action from the prism of the desired outcome. This is a stage of "reframing"—an opportune moment to generate new, hopefully more fitting, interventions to engage others in dialogue. The second learning loop restarts the cycle, and so on down the list until the desired outcome is achieved.

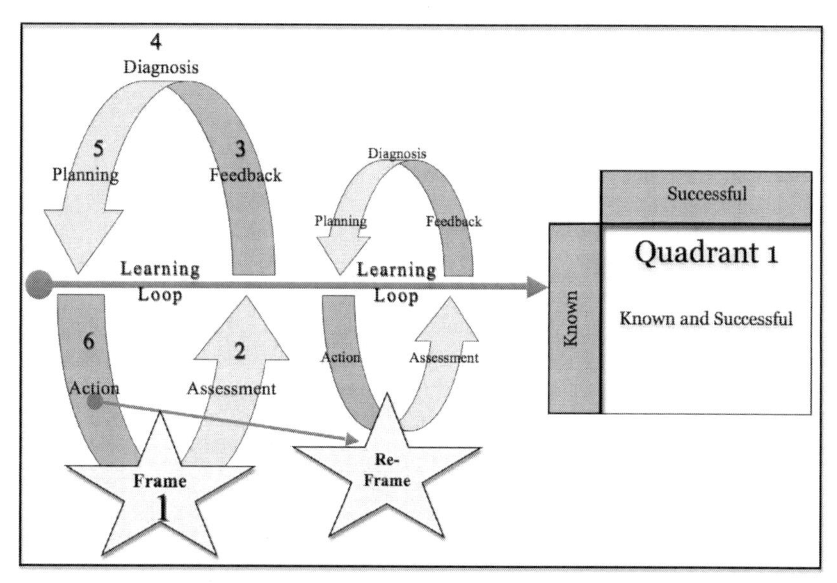

Figure 10.2. Action Research Cycle

Action research is a systematic way to find the coveted quadrant 1, which represents the results that can be safely repeated. It zigzags from theory to action to reflection, until those results are obtained. What makes it so dynamic is it's done in the thick of action.

Step #1: Frame

In their definitive work, Lee Bolman and Terrence Deal (2003) likened the concepts of "framing" and "reframing," used figuratively, to windows, maps, tools, lenses, orientations, and perspectives. Framing and reframing were essentially the mental schemes of people to locate themselves within a particular environment.

When a problem is framed, it becomes logical. School leaders make sense of their schools through a host of mental models expressing the diversity manifested concretely in experience. Aiming toward a successful, resilient school, the foundational leader takes account of this experience and brings meaning to "frames," corresponding to the four key foundations process constructs offered in the preceding chapters:

Frame #1: Listening to People and the Environment A Balancing Process
Frame #2: Building Agreements: A Continuous Process
Frame #3: Co-Creating Purpose: A Step-by-Step Process
Frame #4: Fostering Effective Teams: A Proverbial Process

The foundational leader makes the most of each of the foundational frames and inspires others to *reframe* by proposing activities that promise new insights into their school's transformation.

Step #2: Assessment

This segment requires the collection of data based on series of interviews, focus groups, observations, or structuring devices that can help the school find the best solution. Or it involves an assessment tool like the Four Key Foundations Assessment to be explained later.

The data collected on a current state of affairs have to be disclosed to the school members. Keeping members from the data may give the impression the school is nothing more than smoke and mirrors. The foundational leader is always open and honest about these matters. Whatever the nature of the data, this can be an opportunity for learning.

The stages of diagnosis, planning, and action may take several forms, which the leader has to fit into a series of face-to-face meetings—depending on the employees' needs and the time available.

Step #3: Diagnosis

"Diagnosis" takes the data analysis to a higher level. Once the feedback data have been properly gathered, the Situation in Need of Attention (SITNA) should be clearer. The SITNA represents the discrepancy between the current condition and the desired state—much like the doctor's prognosis after the tests have helped him identify the cause of the illness. Without some understanding of the disorder, the doctor would be at a loss to prescribe the appropriate treatment. The ailment may be as simple as the common flu. A diagnosis allows the doctor to inform the patient of the need to drink lots of fluids and rest.

Like a doctor, the foundational leader cannot afford to wander aimlessly seeking the right intervention. Accurate information is necessary. Using the assessment data presented, including those from the environment, the foundational leader determines the diagnosis. These actions may be described as "triangulation" because the data are pulled from multiple sources of information. Triangulation matches the diagnosis to the dysfunction or SITNA.

Step #4: Planning and Action

With the data gathered and the SITNA established, the foundational leader's task is to bring the employees together for planning and action. Here, inclusive meeting designs and problem-solving techniques are employed from a different perspective. At this advanced phase of the action research, stakeholder involvement is important.

A resource is the six-step approach to effective decision-making and problem-solving described in *The Practical Decision Maker* (Harvey, Bearley, and Corkrum, 2001). It consists of systematic techniques to help facilitators bring together people in the school to generate, winnow, and select ideas in a sound decision-making process.

1. Mindset
2. Problem Definition
3. Solution Criteria
4. Possible Solutions
5. Solution Choice
6. Implementation

"Mindset," analogous to *framing*, sets the stage and identifies the context of the problem. With the diagnosis made possible by action research, the foundational leader leads his or her members through the next step, "problem definition." This demands additional time from the group because the leader must determine if the recognized SITNA is, in fact, the correct area of concern. The "solution criteria" gives the group an opportunity to establish needs, wants, and available resources.

The group is now positioned to take the next steps, generating "possible solutions" and "solution choice." This is an opportunity to apply a variety of techniques, which not only assist groups in producing different solutions, but also helps them winnow the list of possible solutions.

The foundational leader moves the selected solutions into the arena of action called "implementation," the last stage of the learning cycle. To keep the action plans manageable, the foundational leader works with the school members to develop S.M.A.R.T. goals (Specific, Measurable, Attainable, Results-Oriented, and Timely), a term popularized by Richard DuFour et al.'s (2006) work on professional learning communities.

Figure 10.3 below displays a S.M.A.R.T. goal worksheet, which the school can employ as a vehicle to action. It has five columns—goal, specific steps, responsibility, timeline, and evidence of effectiveness—each having room for distinct strategies.

The foundational leader implements all the actions worked out through the action research process, while continuing to listen to people, pay attention to the environment, and document emerging data. When the actions have run their course more or less within their allotted timelines, the first learning loop effectively comes to an end.

The actions implemented so far have either had a positive impact on the SITNA or at least are known to have produced the current state. The objective is both to overcome the barriers to success and to grasp how each step taken has contributed to the new situation.

The foundational leader embarks on the second learning loop by reframing and repeating each of the steps from *The Practical Decision Maker*. These learning loops continue until he or she and his or her constituents are satisfied with the outcome—in other words, when the SITNA is no longer a SITNA.

S.M.A.R.T. GOAL WORKSHEET

SPECIFIC...MEASURABLE...ATTAINABLE...RESULTS-ORIENTED...TIMELY

Situation in Need of Attention (SITNA):		School/Team:		Date:
Data & Goal	**Steps/Strategies**	**Responsibility**	**Timeline**	**Evidence of Effectiveness**
Goal:	1. 2. 3.	1. 2. 3.	1. 2. 3.	

Figure 10.3. S.M.A.R.T. Goal Worksheet

THE FOUR KEY FOUNDATIONS ASSESSMENT

The Four Key Foundations Assessment (fig. 10.4) is designed to assess employee perceptions regarding the four key foundations. The school may already demonstrate evidence of one or some of the foundations, but at a maturity level that does not yet allow the foundation a firm role in creating resilience.

The survey helps establish the evidence (or lack thereof). This evidence assists the foundational leader in creating the necessary intervention to move the school toward greater resilience.

PROGRESSIVE PRACTITIONER IN ACTION

In the following example of a leader's action research, a series of activities are attached to the six phases of the action-research model.

Four Key Foundations Assessment

Directions: This instrument assesses your perceptions about the current reality of your school. Read each statement and then use the scale below to select the score that best reflects your personal degree of agreement with the statement. Be certain to select only one response for each statement. The first three sections (Listening to the People and the Environment, Building Agreements, and Co-Creating Purpose) focus on the school in general. The last section (Fostering Effective Teams) is aimed at determining information about the team(s) with which you belong.

Scale:
1 = Strongly Disagree 2 = Disagree 3 = Agree 4 = Strongly Agree

Foundation #1: Listening to People and the Environment	*1*	*2*	*3*	*4*
1. The leader frequently listens to staff members to seek ideas and input on key decisions.				
2. Meetings are regularly used to effectively make decisions and accomplish important tasks.				
3. The leader is able to sense when problems arise (both internal and external) and is proactive in addressing those problems.				
4. When staff members have a concern the leader listens and takes appropriate action in a timely manner.				
5. The leader participates democratically with staff members in the sharing of decision-making authority.				
6. When important decisions are made the leader consistently communicates the reasoning behind those decisions.				
7. Decisions are regularly made based on current data and information.				
8. The staff has frequent opportunities to formally and informally share ideas and suggestions for improvement.				
9. Everyone supports decisions even though they may not agree with them.				
10. Everyone assumes shared responsibility and accountability in important decisions without evidence of imposed power and authority.				

Foundation #2: Building Agreements	*1*	*2*	*3*	*4*
11. The staff's actions and behaviors are built on trust, respect and caring relationships.				
12. The staff perceives conflict and tension as an opportunity for growth.				
13. Differences of opinion between staff members exist and are discussed openly.				
14. Staff is comfortable communicating feelings and frustrations.				
15. When conflict or tension arises, each staff member addresses it in a constructive manner.				
16. The staff has formally established productive norms and commitments that define the way everyone should behave.				
17. The staff knows of and accepts the agreed upon behaviors and commitments.				
18. The staff consistently confronts those who are not following through with agreed upon behaviors and commitments.				
19. When changes occur (e.g., new members arrive, restructuring, initiatives, etc.) the staff regularly revisits the agreed upon behaviors and makes changes when necessary.				
20. The leader's actions always exemplify agreed upon behaviors and commitments.				

Foundation #3: Co-Creating Purpose	*1*	*2*	*3*	*4*
21. The staff functions with a strong sense of commitment and shared purpose.				
22. There exists a realistic and compelling vision and mission with recognizable goals that serve as guideposts.				
23. The accomplishment of short-term goals is celebrated often.				
24. The staff's actions are aligned with the vision, mission and goals.				
25. Each staff member's personal values, goals and aspirations are known and recognized.				
26. Each staff member's personal values, goals and aspirations are somehow interconnected with the overarching collective purpose.				
27. A collaborative process exists for developing shared purpose and commitment among the staff.				
28. The staff places the collective purpose on par with their personal ambitions.				
29. The leader regularly articulates and communicates the vision, mission and goals.				
30. Teams are focused and work interdependently to achieve the joint vision, mission and recognizable goals.				

Figure 10.4. Four Key Foundations Assessment

Foundation #4: Fostering Effective Teams	*1*	*2*	*3*	*4*
31. Team members share a common identity and work from a common set of beliefs.				
32. Team members work together (as opposed to working in isolation) in order to accomplish tasks.				
33. Feelings of trust exist within the team and among its members.				
34. The team's work environment is joyful or positive.				
35. Conflict among team members is openly dealt with; it is not allowed to fester.				
36. Team discourse surrounds high levels of listening and question asking.				
37. Risk-taking is encouraged while errors are tolerated and seen as opportunities for growth.				
38. Team members understand and accept the group's organizational structure and operational format.				
39. The group engages in periodic "time out" or "maintenance sessions" to address individual concerns about processes or behaviors.				
40. The team is aware of external factors and is pragmatic in its approach.				

Figure 10.4. (***continued***)

The context is a large school with a diverse student population. Approximately 93 percent of the students receive free and reduced lunch, reflecting the elevated poverty rate of the surrounding community. In the past few years, the school has been ineffective in closing the achievement gap; Caucasian students have continued to outscore their counterparts at alarming rates. In view of the entrenched culture, the newly hired school principal decides to spend a couple of months observing and talking to everyone in the hope of identifying specific problems.

One problem he sees is teacher isolation. Although teachers want to work together, they don't know how. The principal can impose time for activities to force them to collaborate. Instead of taking this autocratic approach, he chooses to bring them together to explore the four key foundations to allow them to raise their understanding of the necessary skills and mindset of effective collaboration.

Assuming responsibility for framing the situation with respect to each foundation, he determines:

- Framing Foundation #1: Listening to People and the Environment. The previous principal ran a tight ship. He was a prime example of the command-and-control leadership style and had an aggressive approach. People disliked him and filed grievances every time they were asked to do something out of the ordinary. A "leadership team" was supposed to make key decisions for the school, but the principal used the time to forward a personal agenda. There were no opportunities for input on decisions.

- Framing Foundation #2: Building Agreements. The school has no explicitly developed productive group norms. Because teacher isolation is evident, it has become common practice for the teachers to ignore one another. On several occasions, they have argued in the staff lounge over a new program.
- Framing Foundation #3: Co-Creating Purpose. On a shelf is the school's vision and mission statement, written four years ago. Since then, there has been no exploration of purpose.
- Framing Foundation #4: Fostering Effective Teams. Teachers are expected to work in teams to analyze information on students and to make decisions. During staff meetings, the teams are required to turn in their work to the principal. A few teams work seamlessly, while others turn in subpar plans to re-teach. Only about 20 percent of them operate to their potential.

This initial frame reveals a multitude of SITNAs. However, not all SITNAs can be tackled at once. Building a successful, resilient school by focusing on the four key foundations may take years.

During the next staff meeting, the principal moves to the assessment stage of his action research and hands out the Four Key Foundations Assessment. In his analysis of the data, he finds many of the areas of the assessment scored lower than he expected. The average response was "disagree," indicating little or no foundations were in evidence.

At the next meeting (feedback), he shares this finding with the staff and asks small groups for further discussion of the data. Later, during group presentations, the principal jots their responses on a large poster paper, placing each idea under the appropriate rubric.

The teachers agree the foundations need attention and express the desire to begin with the first foundation–listening to people and the environment. During a heated debate, they make clear their frustration at never being heard. "We have good ideas if you just give us the opportunity," they say. The principal and his staff agree on the urgency to developing listening. They also speak to the importance of building agreements.

At the next leadership meeting, the principal provides further background on each of the four key foundations, along with some ideas culled from the available literature for everyone to read in order to set the next stage. Since the aim of this meeting is to find solutions and develop a plan for implementation, he references *The Practical Decision Maker* to facilitate the steps needed. He suggests specific methods for building or rebuilding the foundations.

This process proves very constructive. They vote according to the spend-a-dot method, where the voters cast their vote on the ideas they like best using circular stickers. The voting results help decide, among other things, two activities to improve the two foundational areas of listening and building agreements:

- Strategy #1: A two-day retreat is planned for the next pedagogical break where the staff will participate in a large-group process called open space technology. This gives everyone an opportunity to express input on aspects of schooling about which he or she feels most passionate. The data obtained from this event will be used throughout the school year to make decisions.
- Strategy #2: The staff creates and agrees on productive group norms during their next staff meeting. As a starting point, this activity lasts one hour. Within the frame of building agreements as a continuous process, developing productive group norms has to be an ongoing activity.

Next, the leadership team puts these actions on paper by completing a S.M.A.R.T. goal, marking the conclusion of the first learning loop in the action research process. Figure 10.5 below outlines the S.M.A.R.T. goal developed by the leadership team. The goal's implementation constitutes a critical starting point. The next learning loop can consider either the second Four Key Foundations Assessment completed by the staff or its response to other emerging data.

This work does not end the story. Action research is ongoing, and the project may take many years before it runs its course. In this example, the principal strives to use data in the execution of strategies to move each foundation into an actionable phase. This is how

S.M.A.R.T. Goal Worksheet

Specific...Measurable...Attainable...Results-oriented...Timely

Situation in Need of Attention (SITNA): OFQ #1 – Listening to the School & Building Agreements		**School**		**Date:**
Data & Goal	**Steps/Strategies**	**Responsibility**	**Timeline**	**Evidence of Effectiveness**
• The area on the Key Foundations Assessment #1 with the second least mean (2.78) was, *Listening to the People and the Environment.* • The area on the Key Foundations Assessment #1 with the overall least mean (2.63) was, *Building Agreements.* **Goal:** Following a sequence of activities, the expected outcome is for each of the above-mentioned areas to score a mean above 3.0 on the Key Foundations Assessment #2. This goal denotes the staff, as a whole, agrees that each of the two areas is present in the school.	1. A two-day retreat will be planned during the break in May. During this retreat, the staff will participate in the large-group process Open Space Technology. The principal will use the data to make many of the future decisions. 2. The staff will create and agree upon productive group norms. This activity will encompass each staff member writing the behavior that they want to see on a 3x5 index card. All cards will be collected and placed on the wall based on the area it addresses. Each staff member will get 5 Spend-a-dots and vote on the behaviors they most value.	1. Administration and the Leadership Team will develop the agenda and discuss logistics at the next Leadership Team meeting. 2. Three Leadership Team members agreed to facilitate the meeting. The principal will get the members all the materials that they need.	1. The timeline will be completed following the next Leadership Team Meeting. 2. The newly developed group norms will be developed at the next staff meeting. The principal will have them posted in workrooms within a week after they are developed.	• Increase in means for the items on the Key Foundations Assessment #2. • Informal and formal feedback from members of the school.

Figure 10.5. Leadership Team S.M.A.R.T. Goal

the foundational leader facilitates action research and becomes a progressive practitioner.

By the end of the first year, the principal creates a flourishing culture where his school is headed towards success and resiliency because everyone finally knows and understands the importance of the four key foundations. Since the first staff meeting, where everyone completed the first four key foundations assessment, the staff participated in four learning loops.

The most recent survey indicated significant progress in each loop. In fact, the average combined scores for listening to the organization and building agreements holds fast at the category of "agreed."

At this point, everyone generally feels it's time to develop co-creating purpose as the next foundation. They plan to participate in a process called Future Search Conference, where they tap into individual purposes to create a collective purpose they can call their own.

Success is happening, and the principal knows exactly what actions led to it. These two aspects are what make the foundational leader a progressive practitioner.

With respect to action research, the foundational leader establishes or reestablishes school health by treating specific dysfunction. For this, the foundational leader has to measure the school's present state against the desired state, just as any medical practitioner would.

The school simply has to grow and evolve. After diagnosis, the foundational leader develops a plan for an effective intervention and follow-up.

At every stage, school goals are continually changing, which, in turn, keeps the desired state of the school malleable and subject to change. The status quo, no matter how comfortable, is simply not an option. The foundational leader continually measures the temperature of the school by listening to and allowing others to give their open and honest feedback.

If the four key foundations are not properly maintained in this way, the members are almost certain to perceive the desired state as an imposition from above.

AMPUTATE WHEN NECESSARY

Before moving to the concluding chapter, "Final Thoughts," it is essential to leave a long-lasting impression about the seriousness of moving the four key foundations forward. It is a brutal declaration, but needs to be said.

Throughout the process of nurturing the four key foundations through action research, some refuse to give in and resist. It is a part of change. Whether the source is burnout or stubbornness, it is the foundational leader's responsibility to take every measure to change their outlook so they do not impede ongoing progress.

If, after varied interventions, there is still no hope of getting an insubordinate member back on track, the foundational leader will consider amputation—in other words, documentation leading to dismissal. It is a last resort, but it will prove farsighted.

The foundational leader is responsible for setting the tone. Inaction is itself a kind of intervention, albeit one with the clear message: Mediocrity is our policy!

11

FINAL THOUGHTS

If you don't create change, change will create you.

—Unknown

Schools evolve continuously. With each passing day, some get stronger, while others spiral downward toward certain demise. Economic conditions can be merciless. The single most important lesson to be learned is those schools that meet success happen also to be the ones that take the time to lay the four key foundations properly. Their success is built on the engagement of the whole school community. These are the elements of a successful school able to overcome adversity.

The time for change is always now. The true foundational leader has to cut the Gordian Knot to free the school of its dysfunctional past. In this task, there is always a beginning and an end to every cycle; the secret is in keeping the process of renewal going as long as the school exists.

Foundational leaders create schools almost like self-cleaning ovens. Their staff has the capacity to respond effectively to chaos because they have created a culture that wants to sparkle in the midst of chaos. Their focus is on the four key foundations, without which the future would not look promising.

In trying times like now, schools are flipped upside-down, bent out of shape, and stretched to the limit. They take a real beating. But it's *never* too late to take the helm. The foundation leader has to do it in more ways than just in an officiating capacity.

That's what makes him or her a foundational school leader.

REFERENCE LIST

Bennis, W., and B. Nanus. 2005. *Leaders: Strategies for taking charge*. New York: First Collins Business Essentials.

Bolman, L., and T. Deal. 2003. *Reframing organizations: Artistry, choice, and leadership*. San Francisco, CA: Jossey-Bass.

Brown, J. 2005. *The world café: Shaping our futures through conversation that matters*. San Francisco, CA: Berrett-Koehler.

Bunker, B., and B. Alban. 1997. *Large group interventions: Engaging the whole system for rapid change*. San Francisco, CA: Jossey-Bass.

———. 2006. *The handbook of large group methods: Creating systemic change in organizations and communities*. San Francisco, CA: Jossey-Bass.

Corkrum, R. 1996. Using team characteristics to predict teamness: Validation of the Harvey/Drolet construct. EdD diss., University of La Verne. (UMI No. 9708874).

Covey, S., and R. Merrill. 2006. *The speed of trust: The one thing that changes everything*. New York: Free Press.

DuFour, R. P., R. B. DuFour, R. Eaker, and T. Many. 2006. *Learning by doing: A handbook for professional learning communities at work*. Bloomington, IN: Solution Tree.

Fullen, M. 2001. *Leading in a culture of change.* San Francisco, CA: Jossey-Bass.

Harvey, T., W. Bearley, and S. Corkrum. 2001. *The practical decision maker.* Lanham, MD: Scarecrow Education.

Harvey, T., and B. Drolet. 2004. *Building teams, building people: Expanding the fifth resource.* Lanham, MD: Scarecrow Education.

Heifetz, R., and M. Linsky. 2002. *Leadership on the line: Staying alive through the dangers of leading.* Boston: Harvard Business School Press.

Holman, P., T. Devane, and S. Cady. 2007. *The change handbook: The definitive resource on today's best methods for engaging whole systems.* San Francisco, CA: Berrett-Koehler.

Keene, M., and B. Erford. 2007. *Group activities: Firing up for performance.* Saddle River, NJ: Pearson Education.

Klatt, B. 1999. *The ultimate training workshop handbook: A comprehensive guide to leading successful workshops and training programs.* New York: McGraw-Hill.

Kouzes, J., and B. Posner. 2002. *Leadership: The challenge.* 3rd ed. New York: Jossey-Bass.

LaFasto, F., and C. Larson. 2001. *When teams work best.* Thousand Oaks, CA: Sage Publications.

Levi, D. 2001. *Group dynamics of teams.* Thousand Oaks, CA: Sage Publications.

Liteman, M., S. Campbell, and J. Liteman. 2006. *Retreats that work: Everything you need to know about planning and leading great offsites.* San Francisco, CA: Pfeiffer.

Maslow, A. 1943. A theory of human motivation. *Psychological Review.* 50:370–96. Retrieved June 8, 2009, from http://psychclassics.yorku.ca/Maslow/motivation.htm.

Maurer, R. 2004. *One small step can change your life: The kaizen way.* New York: Workman.

Michalko, M. 2006. *Thinkertoys: A handbook of creative thinking techniques.* Berkeley, CA: Ten Speed Press.

Newstrom, J., and E. Scannell. 1998. *The big book of teambuilding games: Trust-building activities, team spirit exercises, and other fun things to do.* New York: McGraw-Hill.

Nilson, C. 1993. *Team games for trainers: High-involvement games and training aids for developing these and other team skills.* New York: McGraw-Hill.

Owen, H. 1997a. *Open space technology: A user's guide.* San Francisco, CA: Berrett-Koehler.

———. 1997b. *Expanding our now: The story of open space technology.* San Francisco, CA: Berrett-Koehler.

Pfeiffer, J., and J. Jones. 1978. *The 1978 annual handbook for group facilitators.* San Diego, CA: Pfeiffer and Company.

Schwartz, R. 2002. *The skilled facilitator: A comprehensive resource for consultants, facilitators, managers, trainers, and coaches.* San Francisco, CA: Jossey-Bass.

Silberman, M. 1999. *101 ways to make meetings active: Surefire ideas to engage your group.* San Francisco, CA: Jossey-Bass.

Tuckman, B. 1965. Developmental sequence in small groups. *Psychological Bulletin.* 63:384–99. Reprinted in *Group Facilitation: A Research and Applications Journal* (Number 3, Spring 2001) and available as a Microsoft Word document: http://dennislearningcenter.osu.edu/references/GROUP%20DEV%20ARTICLE.doc. (accessed June 7, 2009).

Ulrich, D. 1996. Credibility x capability. In *The leader of the future,* ed. F. Hesselbein, M. Goldsmith, and R. Beckhard, 209–20. San Francisco, CA: Jossey-Bass.

Weisbord, M., and S. Janoff. 1995. *Future search: An action guide to finding common ground in organizations and communities.* San Francisco, CA: Berrett-Koehler.

West, E. 1996. *201 icebreakers: Group mixers, warm-ups, energizers, and playful activities.* New York: McGraw-Hill.

Whitworth, L., H. Kimsey-House, and P. Sandahl. 1998. *Co-active coaching: New skills for coaching people toward success in work and life.* Mountain View, CA: Davies-Black Publishing.

Wilkinson, M. 2004. *The secrets of facilitation: The S.M.A.R.T. guide to getting results with groups.* San Francisco, CA: Jossey-Bass.

ABOUT THE AUTHOR

Perry P. Wiseman is a middle school principal in the San Bernardino City Unified School District in San Bernardino, California. He recently opened a new school and had the fond opportunity to bring together a new staff and co-create a school culture built with the fundamental foundations outlined in this book. He received his doctorate in organizational leadership from the University of La Verne and an M.A. in educational leadership from the University of Redlands. His award-winning dissertation study examined professional learning communities and the effectiveness of the teams within those communities. Dr. Wiseman spends his free time with his wife and two sons, Samantha, Nick, and Matthew. He is working to launch WiseFoundations, a new consulting firm that concentrates on strategic planning and effective change in schools.

SUNY BROCKPORT
3 2815 00912 1990